THE CONRAN HOME DECOR

CURTAINS
AND BLINDS

THE CONRAN HOME DECORATOR
CURTAINS
AND BLINDS

CAROLINE CLIFTON-MOGG

VILLARD BOOKS
NEW YORK 1986

Please note. The photographs have been collected
from all over the world to show as varied a range
of ideas as possible within the scope of this
book, so that not all the items featured are
available through Conran's.

All rights reserved under International and Pan-American Copyright Conventions.
Published in the United States by Villard Books, a division of Random House, Inc.,
New York, and simultaneously in Canada by Random House of Canada Limited, Toronto.
First published in Great Britain by Conran Octopus Limited.

Conceived, designed and produced by
Conran Octopus Limited
28-32 Shelton Street
London WC2 9PH

Project editor: Liz Wilhide
Art editor: Jane Willis
Designer: Gunna Finnsdottir
Picture research: Keith Bernstein
Additional editorial assistance: Dorothea Hall and Hilary More

Library of Congress Catalog Card Number: 85-45451
ISBN: 0-394-74397-0

Printed and bound in Hong Kong
9 8 7 6 5 4 3 2
First American Edition

CONTENTS

WINDOW DRESSING

Windows are such a necessary part of any room that, ironically, they are frequently taken for granted, and often even ignored. But as practical and decorative assets, windows are all-important in the scheme of things – light, air, and sunshine are all essential to our mental well-being while windows are our link with the outside world.

All windows are functional, and that can be combined with as little or as much decoration as you like, and since the window is such an integral part of any room it could become a major element in your overall scheme: a decorative opportunity not to be missed.

So stand back and take a look. What do you want from those particular windows. Should they stand out or blend in? Some windows look best left alone, others need curtains and blinds to emphasize their shape, while some – great view, pity about the shape, and vice versa – cry out for disguise.

Today there is more fabric choice than ever before. From rough wools and tweeds through to splashy chintz and see-through voiles. So somewhere there is something that is just right for you and your window.

An essential part of the decorating process, and one not to be rushed, is choosing which sort of treatment is best for your windows. Warmth, privacy and light are all practical considerations which should be taken into account. Remember, also, that windows and rooms look different in different lights. So notice the way the light falls, both morning and evening, in sunshine and cloud, before taking a final decision about fabric.

When working with fabric always remember that the important areas in which not to skimp are those which are most precious – time and thought. Small details count; in fact, detail is really what it is all about.

A simple but stunning idea for a contemporary setting. A plain unlined curtain acts as both window and wall covering.

PRACTICAL USES

Right: Where sun and air are the most vital elements in a room, there is no virtue in over-complicating matters. Here, a long curtain in a textured fabric makes an ideal room divider.

Although most people want curtains and blinds to look good they usually have to fulfill a number of useful functions as well. Their insulating qualities, for example, are just as welcome in today's heated homes as they were when rooms were much draftier. When choosing a window covering, bear in mind what functions you want it to perform.

Privacy

Privacy is a precious commodity everywhere, but particularly in bedrooms, bathrooms and lavatories, and in places that are directly overlooked. Venetian and other slatted blinds which can be adjusted to give varying degrees of light and total blackout at night are ideal for all of these locations.

For privacy in bedrooms and living rooms, the traditional solutions are full-length sheers, single or tiered café curtains, or heavy lace with lined curtains. You can also use blinds on their own or with curtains, but remember that neither fabric nor cane blinds provide total privacy, especially at night when the room is well lit.

Insulation

All curtains and blinds will keep out cold and noise to a certain extent and help with the fuel bills – but not if the windows themselves are ill-fitting. Apart from installing double-glazing, the most effective insulation is to hang interlined curtains made from a heavyweight fabric and extend them well beyond the window frame. There are also various aluminum-coated interlinings and acrylic-coated linings available.

Light exclusion

For children who find it difficult to go to sleep in daylight, or light sleepers, natural light may need to be cut out to a high degree. Both interlined curtains and blinds made in very dark colors such as bottle green, navy blue and chocolate brown will help prevent light penetrating. If using curtains in a dark fabric, buy a lining fabric in a dark toning color. To exclude light totally, line curtains with blackout fabric or the new white or cream acrylic-coated linings, which cut out light very effectively, as well as reducing heat loss.

Roller blinds make stylish cover-ups. The bright color and clean lines mean that eating in this room is a pleasure – free from the worry about what debris might lurk behind the screen.

Room separation

Large rooms that are used for several different functions can be partitioned off by properly positioned curtains or blinds. Fixtures can be suspended from the ceiling to support either louvers, slatted wood, matchstick or Venetian blinds. To allow the maximum amount of light to penetrate use sheer or open-weave fabrics. If available light is not a problem the choice of fabric is limitless. If the lightweight fabrics have a tendency to wave about, weight the hem edge either with disc-shaped weights, positioned at each base corner and at the base of each seam, or run a length of covered weights inside the hem crease. Curtain dividers should be avoided in kitchen areas as fabric easily absorbs cooking smells and grease. However, the stiffened fabric that is used for roller blinds can be wiped to remove any unsightly marks.

Concealing storage

Both curtains and blinds make effective screening for storage areas and protect the contents from dust and light. Clothes hung on a rail in a bedroom alcove can be covered with pretty unlined curtains or a ceiling-to-floor blind if there is no room for cupboard doors. When positioned across alcoves the area can be outlined with a decorative molding, painted to match the color scheme of the room, then the roller blind will fit neatly in position, with the edging holding it in place.

Study areas could be made less obvious if you hide shelves above a desktop behind a plain roller blind. Similarly, curtaining an understair space could transform it into a useful storage area. In these positions, use a crenellated edge and a length of dowel, to provide a hand hold, as opposed to a cord and "acorn".

DECORATIVE USES

The decorative elements of curtains and blinds go a long way beyond merely matching other pieces in the room. Over coordination, in any case, is a plague to be avoided. It is important to incorporate the window into the overall decorative scheme, but remember that the way a window is treated can affect the proportions, the style and the very atmosphere of a room.

Style

Curtains and blinds play an important role in pulling a look together. The wrong type of curtain heading or a glaringly modern blind, for example, can strike a note of discord in the most carefully reconstructed period interior. A fussy festoon blind or formal dress curtains would be just as out of place in a contemporary setting. But between these extremes there are nuances which you must be aware of when planning a decorative scheme.

Atmosphere

The mood of an interior is highly influenced by the quality and amount of natural light. Unfortunately, few rooms can boast an even, gentle diffusion of light; awkwardly placed windows or a poor aspect can create conditions ranging from harsh glare to permanent semi-gloom. Carefully chosen fabrics and window treatments will go a long way towards improving such a dismal prospect.

   Cold, harsh light can be filtered with Venetian blinds or other slatted blinds made of wood, cane or bamboo. Sheers, the traditional remedy for softening glaring light, can be made in white, or a pale shade for a warmer look.

   Where there is too little light in a room, make the most of what you do get by using pale-colored fabrics with smooth or shiny surfaces that will reflect light, and take the curtains beyond the window on an extended track, holding them away from the frame with tie-backs.

Making the most of views

Where there is something worth looking at, the window treatment should be kept plain and simple, the window acting

Bring down the window width by hanging the curtains so they permanently meet in the center. Hold them back with tie-backs.

On tall, narrow windows hang full-length curtains on a track or pole extended out well beyond the sides of the windows.

On short windows, add height by fixing the pole or track high above the window and adding floor-length curtains.

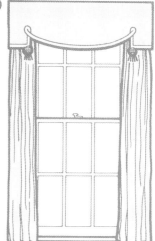

Adding a deep decorative-edge pelmet over the top of long curtains will help to reduce the height of a tall window.

Plain, simple and very striking, these floor-length, shocking pink and loosely woven curtains bathe the room in a rosy light. So often window treatments just melt into the background, but there is no reason why they should not become features in their own right.

as an extended frame around a picture. A pretty valance, for example, could be used above an arched window with a secluded outlook, or an asymmetric swag draped to balance a tall tree or building.

An ugly view presents a different problem. While it is important to distract from the scene outside, you can rarely block out all the window light. Exclude the view but keep the light by choosing one of the many colorful slatted blinds available (including louvered panels and plywood screens with designs of punched holes). Or choose one of the new, highly individual patterned nets which can be bought in a variety of depths and hues.

Café curtains hung with brightly colored poles and rings will also distract the eye from the view.

Visual tricks

Curtains and blinds can be used in several ways to correct certain architectural faults. Carefully dressed windows, doors and alcoves can give an impression of increased or reduced height or width.

The height of a window can be reduced with a café curtain, a deep pelmet, valance or draped swags and tails, while alcoves and openings can be made to seem less high with an asymmetric curtain draped permanently across. Windows can be made to look wider by extending the length of the curtain track or width of the blind beyond the actual opening. Striped floor-length curtains will suggest greater height in a low-ceilinged room; and sill-length curtains patterned in a horizontal design will make a high ceiling seem lower.

CURTAINS OR BLINDS

Whether you cover windows with curtains or blinds – or both – is a question of what you like and how much you want to spend. Also there are certain situations and types of window where only curtains will work, and others where blinds would be the best solution.

The reasons are chiefly to do with the proportions of the window, and of the room. Curtains really only work at two lengths – sill length and floor length (and these days it is fashionable to make them longer than floor length). With a small window set high, sill-length curtains would look ridiculous, and curtains that fell to the floor would use a large amount of fabric, making the window appear far too important for its size. In this case, only a blind would do. Similarly, windows that are wider than usual often look better covered with curtains because blinds that are much wider than their height may lose their neatness and precision of line, and tend to bag or wave.

Cost

As the expense of covering all the windows in a home is high, and large windows cost more to cover than small ones, your decisions should be considered carefully to avoid making expensive mistakes. On the whole, most blinds are cheaper than most curtains. It is a good idea to choose less expensive window coverings for kitchens, bathrooms, children's rooms and workrooms – save the more expensive ones for living areas, main bedrooms and entrance halls.

Suitability of fabric

As shops are usually loath to give you large samples of fabric, or let you fiddle with it seeing how it drapes and falls, it is often hard for you to imagine what it will look like when made up. So buy the smallest quantity if it is an expensive fabric – 4 inches is usually the least you can buy – or invest in a yard or so if it is relatively cheap (you can always use it to make cushions, tie-backs or a pelmet or valance) and take it home to hang beside the relevant window. This will enable you to see what the fabric looks like in different lights, and it gives you a chance to live with it.

Roman blinds look good in plain colors – perhaps trimmed or edged with a braid or a decorative border – all treatments that emphasize the blind's geometric qualities. But they can also be made up in a fabric with a small overall design, or a geometric one, as can roller blinds.

Feminine festoon blinds, on the other hand, require quite different treatment. The loose curves of the festoon lend themselves to designs that would work as well on a curtain, such as floral prints, or smallish abstracts. If you do choose a splashy pattern, cut down on the frills.

Floor-length curtains can take bold designs – the sort of pattern that has a large repeat. Sill-length curtains look best if the design is medium-sized and not too overpowering. The ever-popular floral patterns and large abstracts also work

well on curtains – better than on blinds. Plain fabrics, too, can be effective. On floor-length curtains it is a good idea to break up the expanse of color with either a trim in a contrasting shade down the sides and across the bottom, or with contrasting tie-backs.

Then there are stripes. Striped patterns look dramatic and graphic on a Roman or roller blind, unfussy on a festoon blind, fresh and bright on sill-length curtains and elegant on long curtains. From traditional narrow Regency stripes to wide bands of color, there is one for every style of window.

Today, there is more fabric choice than ever before. From rough wools and tweeds through to splashy chintz and see-through voiles. So, somewhere, there is something that is just right for you and your home.

Above: If you are looking for a plain but interesting window treatment for a kitchen use Roman blinds, which will continue the clean, uncluttered lines of the kitchen units.

Left: The gently gathered, pearl-grey curtains in this attic study/bedroom soften but do not detract from the unusual roof angles. Wooden poles and matching rings hold the curtains in place over both the skylight and the main window.

SPECIFIC LOCATIONS

Apart from questions of style, practical issues such as safety and privacy may dictate your choice of window coverings. Curtains or blinds that work well in some locations may prove to be useless, even positively dangerous, in others.

Bathrooms

Both curtain fabric and fittings are prone to condensation in bathrooms. Medium-weight cottons, sheers and toweling are reasonably absorbent fabrics and are ideal for window curtains, and plastic sheeting is ideal for shower curtains.

If the window is not directly over the bath or basin, the curtains should be hung on an extendable track to allow the air to circulate freely. Where the windows are near the bath or basin, curtains should be slightly shorter than the sill, and preferably not too full, to prevent them from becoming splashed with toothpaste or soap. During the day a sheer curtain set well into the window will provide privacy, but it will be virtually transparent at night with artificial light shining behind; a roller blind or lined curtain will be necessary for total screening. Alternatively, use a Venetian blind.

Kitchens

Keep safety in mind when choosing window coverings for kitchens. If the window is anywhere near the cooker or oven, make sure that curtains or blinds cannot touch the heat source at any time. Even if the window is not directly in line with hobs or hotplates, sudden breezes may cause curtains to billow out, so provide secure tie-backs. Blinds are usually a better choice, but only if they can be raised into a safe and neat place.

Another consideration is the constant problem of grease. On the whole, curtains tend to collect more dirt than blinds. Venetian blinds will be easier to clean than roller blinds. Condensation, splashing or spattering may also present

problems if the window is over a sink. Choose fabrics which are either easily washable or wipeable.

Staircases

It is not always necessary to cover staircase windows. If you have to, make sure you take account of safety: heavy curtains may block out too much daylight and blinds on low windows may leave cords trailing near the stairs that could be dangerous in semi-darkness.

Bedrooms and living areas

While bedrooms and living areas are places for you to experiment with new ideas, colors and styles, remember that if you live in the city, curtains will get dirty quickly. If you prefer pale, subtle colors it is wise to pick washable fabrics or else be prepared for having to dry clean them regularly – the cost of dry-cleaning large curtains can be horrendous.

Far left: A red shower curtain that matches the glossy radiator and wall mirror makes this shower room a bright place to start the day.

Left: In this bathroom, the same pattern, used in reverse, is made up into a café curtain and an adaptable vertical roller blind.

Above: Blinds are a good choice for a kitchen since they tend to collect less dirt than curtains and they can easily be raised up out of the way.

Right: A clever idea for a child's room – the blind can be pulled down to provide instant shade for afternoon naps.

LIGHT

The type of curtain or blind you choose can affect the atmosphere of an interior by alternating the quality of the light. Experimenting with different weights and textures of material will reveal a range of subtle and interesting effects. If the light is naturally cold or harsh, filtering it through an open-weave fabric or slatted blind will create soft shadows to take the edge off the glare.

Sheer curtains are the traditional way of making light pleasantly diffused. There are many modern designs but some of the most interesting effects can be produced by using lace. While antique lace is a collector's item found in numerous antique shops, good machine-made repro-ductions are also available from specialist firms and many big stores, either in lengths, panels, or half panels (known as *brise-brise*). Some of the heavier laces, such as Nottingham and Madras (a beautiful gauze-based lace with extra weft threads for building up the surface pattern) can be made into striking roller blinds. Lace or any sheer fabric with a definite pattern can be stretched over a light wooden frame and attached to the window so the full design can be seen clearly.

For a less transparent effect, unlined curtains will allow a certain degree of light through but offer some screening. The color cast over the room by a plain color can be dramatic and intense; a patterned fabric can look soft and luminous.

In the same way, colored or patterned linings can make a striking difference to the quality of light in an interior. Only in the last fifty years or so have people preferred white- or cream-colored lining; before that, curtains were often lined with soft pastel colors or patterned material. A pale pink lining behind an off-white fabric, for example, can warm up steely cold morning light. Make sure, however, that the lining color will not adversely affect the color or pattern of the curtain fabric and result in a peculiar tint.

A window is seen from the outside as well as from inside and it is more fun to come home to interesting-looking windows than a bland, colorless façade. Decorative linings should be chosen with this in mind and coordinated, if possible, with the outside of the house, as well as with the curtains themselves.

Left: In this deceptively simple room, large, completely plain roller blinds play two roles. They act both as permanent diffusers of light, and as a dramatic backdrop for the stylish stools.

Above: These lightweight, translucent curtains have been lined in rich pink. The daylight that diffuses through them is transformed to a soft pink that changes the color of the curtains, the walls and sofa.

COLOR, PATTERN AND TEXTURE

Fabric for curtains and blinds comes in such a wide range of color, pattern and texture that getting it all right, the first time round, can seem a daunting prospect. You can get some outside inspiration by looking closely at rooms designed by professional interior decorators and at those glossy sets featured in interiors magazines and department stores. Many manufacturers also produce their own brochures with ideas on how to use their products and, although often dreary, there is the occasional good idea.

In the world of interior design, as in fashion, colors are usually divided into warm shades – like yellows, pinks and reds – and cool shades – like greens, blues and lilacs – with the addition of the vast family of neutrals – those multitudinous shades that hit all the points between cream, white and grey. If you are thinking about using neutrals, because they seem so safe and easy, bear in mind that because of their very subtlety and underplayed qualities, it needs a very good eye and very confident manner to get the combination right. Neutrals wrongly used just look like different types of dirty white.

Everyone is born with an often subconscious feeling about color, and which colors affect them in which way. Some people feel relaxed in rooms that are shaded green, while others feel despondent. It is important, therefore, not to take the color you want for the windows as an isolated example, but to think of it in terms of the colors you know you can live with – and that can live with you.

Equally important is to take into account how the color at a window will change with the seasons. A sunny yellow will cheer up a room that feels cold and harsh in the winter, but if that window faces south, you may find that the same sunny yellow becomes positively glaring in the height of summer. Keep your more stimulating colors for rooms in which you don't necessarily want to relax, and keep the softer range of colors for rooms in which peace and quiet is of the essence, such as the bedroom. Remember also that the intensity of color will have a strong effect on the proportions of a room. Dark strong colors can make a room look smaller and more enclosed. Lighter colors can make it look larger.

Patterns are tricky. They need to be chosen carefully, and a

certain amount of imagination is required to visualize what a design that seems so smart on a flat panel in the shop will look like when translated into twenty yards of loosely folded curtain at the window.

It's a loose word, pattern. In woven fabrics, it can mean a woven self-patterned design, and on chintzes and cottons it can mean anything from peacocks and pineapples to spots and checks. On the whole, quiet, all-over patterns work better on smaller windows in smaller rooms, and large bold bright patterns work on like-minded windows. Treatment of

the pattern is also important. Large pictorial designs look dreadful on festoon blinds, with all their attendant lace edging and frilling.

If you don't like, or the room can't take, patterns, there is an interesting alternative to be found in using a textured fabric. Visually interesting, without being overpowering, they can work well. Texture can vary from coarse, rough weaves like hessian, to shiny, silky ones like satin; nubbled as in slubbed silk, or deep piled as in velvet. Heavily textured patterns tend to absorb light and smooth shiny ones reflect it.

Above: To hide classically proportioned windows would be a shame. This shuttered pair look wonderful, dressed with plain, rich Austrian blinds.

Left: Every rule is made to be broken, and the feast of color and design here goes to show that you can use more than one pattern – if you dare.

PERIOD STYLE

The past provides a rich source of inspiration, not only for fabric design but also for styles of window dressing. A period look is an obvious choice for homes with a definite historical character, but a less thorough-going approach, picking up on details such as trimmings, can be very effective.

Curtains have been in regular use since the seventeenth century, when they were important for providing both privacy and warmth – excluding drafts, dividing rooms and screening beds. They also played a crucial role in interior decoration, expressing and reflecting changing styles.

The long age of the Georgians saw many different decorative movements come and go, including a rage for designs inspired by Ancient Egypt, but all shared a "classical" sense of harmony and proportion. At the beginning of the era, there was certainly a tendency towards restraint and formality, a mood that prevailed in architecture, interior decoration and dress. Curtains were long and narrow, with dignified swags and ties in light, understated colors.

The Regency period heralded a new flamboyance. Houses were built with much bigger windows to let in more light and air, and the window coverings became more voluminous.

By the middle of Queen Victoria's reign, exuberance in interior decoration had been taken to its extreme. Self-confidence at home and abroad displayed itself in the richness of the interiors. Curtains became fuller and more extravagant, with deeper swags and tails that were often heavily fringed and corded.

Towards the end of the Victorian era, William Morris initiated the Arts and Crafts Movement. Morris aimed to base all his designs for fabric and wallpaper on nature, and his distinctive patterns were immediately successful – and some of them are still being produced.

The twentieth century has also provided more recent material for stylistic borrowing. "Retro" looks such as Art Deco and Fifties modern are particularly popular, not for the style of the curtains themselves but for the vivid and distinctive fabric patterns that we associate with those decades.

Antique curtains

Instead of dressing period windows with modern reproductions, you can try to find original examples. Good eighteenth-century curtains are rare now, but good nineteenth-century curtains can be found at the specialist sales of auction houses. There are also many antique shops and local market stalls that specialize in household textiles.

If the curtains are frayed at the edges, which they often are, a little fabric adhesive applied directly onto the lining works wonders. Original accessories such as cords, tassels and loose fringing will complete the effect.

Far left: If you are lucky enough to possess a perfect antique lace panel, never cut it if it does not fit your window – you will always regret it. If the panel is too long, either fold or loop it as seen here, or drape it. Alternatively, use it on a smaller window, folding it in half and tying back each side either to frame or disguise a view.

Left: For a classic look use a lush, silky textured fabric made up into long, plain curtains which are then loosely held back by rich-looking cords. These rose-colored curtains emphasize but contain the profusion of pattern in the rest of the room.

WINDOW TREATMENTS

The classic window – a perfectly proportioned rectangle beautifully framed by a wooden structure – is rare. Many of the windows in our homes are far from this ideal; they may be small, good at preventing heat loss but bad at letting in light; relatively large, excellent for light but very cold; or an awkward shape altogether.

The first step is to assess what you've got. Stand back and look at the window in isolation, then consider it again in relation to the rest of the room, the color scheme, patterns and textures. The quantity and quality of light is another important factor, and one that will vary dramatically with the time of day.

Curtains and blinds not only affect the appearance of the windows they cover but also alter our perceptions of the proportions of the room as a whole. Floor-length curtains with a pelmet or valance will stress the vertical plane; sill-length ones extended beyond the sides of the window will emphasize the horizontal plane. Softly draped curtains, swagged at the top and swept aside with tie-backs, will disguise hard angles; the clean lines of fine Venetian blinds will contribute a spare, modern look. Vivid colors and bold patterns will draw attention to the window; pastel shades and tiny motifs will help it to blend in.

A further consideration is the view you can see through the window. Don't dress a window in such a way that it fights with a stunning panorama outside; on the other hand, consider leaving sheers, nets or blinds permanently in position if the alternative is a vista of dreary backyards or brick walls.

Most windows could be treated successfully in a number of ways – with simple or elaborate curtains, sheers or nets, and any one of a variety of types of blind. But some impose certain restrictions: blinds are impractical for bow windows, for example. Finally, there are also the windows you should simply leave alone. Where privacy and light are not concerns, beautifully designed windows can be allowed to speak for themselves.

Draperies are becoming increasingly popular and their stylish appearance is surprisingly easy to achieve. Here is a very simple, very cheap, and very romantic treatment for a bedroom. Yards and yards of white muslin fall on to the floor and tumble over it, while more muslin is looped and draped over a plain white wooden pole.

BAYS AND BOWS

Below: A small bow window is best hung with a shaped curtain track, and floor-length curtains that pull back fully at each side, so that the distinction of the shape is enjoyed.

Right: Festoon blinds are eye-catching and romantic – often used in the wrong place, which gives them a fussy reputation. But they are ideal for a small bay window with a pretty view.

Bay windows Although a bay window may comprise as many as six or seven separate panels of glass, it should always be treated as a single unit. If you decide to have curtains, first work out the optimum number. One at each panel will almost certainly be too many, but one at either side of the window may result in a bulky mass when the curtains are drawn back.

The track must be fitted to the shape of the bay: some tracks can be bent; others are sectional and can be taken around any combination of corners; wooden poles can be cut and mitered to make the particular angles required.

Choice of fabric is important since so much of it will be seen. If the bay is very large, a formal arrangement with tie-backs will give a neater look than plain loose curtains. If the windows do not extend to the floor a window seat could be

constructed. Alternatively, treat the bay as a small alcove and enclose it by hanging curtains across the end. If the room is small and you cannot afford to lose the extra space, use roller blinds or fine Venetian blinds.

Bow windows Whatever size it is, a curved window has many of the same curtaining problems as a bay. One draw curtain at either side of the window is probably the best arrangement. You will need to install tracks that can be bent to the appropriate shape. Soft sheers or nets in a simple gathered style can be put up on expandable wires or fine plastic-coated metal rods bent to the correct shape. Blinds, however, are not a practical solution since there are no angles to which they can be attached.

PICTURE AND FRENCH WINDOWS

Picture windows While these large, often wall-sized, windows are excellent for showing off views, they can present certain curtaining problems. Unless the window is double-glazed, for example, there could be excessive heat loss. In this case, full-length curtains made from heavy fabrics will help considerably to conserve heat. For really effective insulation the curtains should also be lined and interlined, and extended beyond the window area to prevent drafts around the edges.

Most picture windows are best covered with simple, full-length curtains, and a textured fabric will provide interest without detracting from the view. To balance the scale of these large curtains it is also usual to use heavier rods and poles with the appropriate rings and brackets.

Where sliding doors are incorporated, it is important to plan the position of the curtains so that when they are drawn back access is clear. This may also involve extending the track beyond the window frame. The whole area can be treated either as one window, or it can be broken with curtains hung at the division points as well as the sides. The curtains should be hung high enough so as not to interfere with the sliding mechanism of the door, or the view.

Far left: A picture window for a sunny, cheerful room adds to the positive atmosphere with a wall of yellow blinds.

Left: A cooler, more elegant decor calls for a plain gathered cotton, which looks sumptuous without detracting from the richness of the furniture.

Depending on the size of the picture window, several styles of blinds can be used effectively. Vertical louvers are an effective choice and they are now available in a wide range of colors.

French windows Evocative of summer days and scented gardens, French windows are glazed doors that open like casements, often on to a garden or terrace. They vary in style and may have double or single doors with smaller windows at each side, and sometimes above. In almost all cases, floor-length curtains give the most pleasing effect, but the important factor is to make sure that the doors can open easily. If the doors of your French window are not the full height of the frame, you can use conventional curtains set high on a decorative pole, which pull back far beyond the doors, otherwise narrow lace panels can be attached to each door frame so that the curtains move with the doors. Slatted wooden blinds, tightly rolled when not in use, give a warm, mellow effect. Painted or stained shutters – whether louvered or otherwise – can look quite good, but make sure that there is enough room for them to fold back. Solid coverings such as these are also useful for security.

DORMERS AND SKYLIGHTS

A pretty and practical idea for dormer windows is to use swivel rods instead of a track. Simply make a casing at the top of each curtain and slide in the rods. To open, swing back the rods and tuck the curtains behind decorative tie-backs.

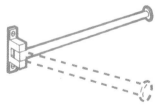

Dormer windows are often small and usually situated in the sloping roof of a house. With such a window, it is best to attach the fittings – whether for curtains or blinds – inside the frame. To get the maximum amount of light, a right-angled, hinged track can be used which will allow the curtains to be drawn back clear of the window.

If the walls of the room are finished in a single color, painting the window frame one or two shades darker will increase the importance and interest of the window. If you want to have fabric blinds or curtains, keep the fabric simple and the pattern in proportion to the size of the window. A pattern that is too large will unbalance the effect – it should be small, neat and well defined. Geometrics, stripes and small designs in bright, crisp fabrics are ideal. As an option you may prefer a wooden blind made from narrow slats.

Clerestory windows are those set high up on a wall, and any covering is difficult. Unless the room is used as a bedroom, and you need to keep out the light, leave well-enough alone. If not, one solution is the Venetian blind. Several varieties are available with a long plastic or Plexiglas rod attached to one edge that extends far below the window, that opens and closes the blinds. Roller and Roman blinds can also be operated from further down the wall. It is important that these windows are simply dressed.

Skylights are windows that are set into roofs. While privacy might not be a problem you may still want to block out some light. This can be effectively filtered by a sheer or net curtain – with plenty of fullness in it – permanently attached between two metal expanding rods or wires. If it is essential to block out the light altogether, special wall fixings are available on which you can mount the rollers of Venetian blinds. Bear in mind, however, that when using a homemade blind covering, the pulley system to open and close the blind will have to be fixed so the blind pulls up the window rather than down. The length of cord involved might also be a problem, so set a large cleat as close to the window as possible to hold the cords neatly, but within easy reach.

Above: Skylights are best left bare, but if a covering is needed either for privacy or a softening effect, sheers with rods slipped through casings top and bottom can be used successfully.

Left: Dormer windows call for more than a little ingenuity. A hinged curtain track is the best solution for many small attic or dormer windows. The curtains cover the area well at night but make the most of available light during the day.

ARCHED AND CIRCULAR WINDOWS

Arched windows are often left bare, but when a covering is necessary it should be sympathetic to the shape. A split Venetian blind is used here, the top part, curved to fit the window arch, is fixed but the lower one can be drawn up independently.

Arched windows can be very beautiful architectural features, and care should be taken to show them off as much as possible, particularly if they are Georgian or Victorian. In old houses they are very often set on a half landing, to light the stairs, and sometimes extend to floor level. In this situation it may be possible to use the window as a frame, for displaying plants or shrubs outside or an attractive arrangement of house plants or a pretty table or chair indoors.

While the ideal solution for an arched window would be to have no covering at all, if it is necessary to cover it – for privacy or warmth – remember to take the decorative curve into account. When deciding on the style of dressing for this type of window, remember that proportion is very important. If the window is tall, any pelmet or valance, whether soft or stiffened, should extend down the sides of the window far enough to balance the height.

A pretty idea for sheers, particularly for a landing window with a shallow arch, would be to have a pelmet or valance made from a pretty printed cotton, with the sheers on an expandable rod beneath it. Sheers or nets could also be used only on the lower half of the window.

If you prefer to have shutters, they can be cut to curve at the top, or used as half-horizontal shutters, giving some insulation and warmth at night.

Round and octagonal windows are striking architectural features which should be left alone. If you are in direct view, and the need for privacy is overwhelming, then substitute, for the clear glass, one of the many types of translucent or sand-blasted glass. These are produced in a variety of designs and textures to suit all types of locations.

Semi-circular windows are not very common, and are usually set high into walls, or above doors to give light to a hallway. In either case, leave the window uncovered. Alternatively, use translucent or stained glass.

Curtain poles above a curved window allow fabric to be drawn well back to reveal the shape. In this case, a recess suggested a theatrical treatment with interlined cotton cut extra long so that the curtains drape attractively. A deep, floppy heading cleverly adds to the softening effect.

PROBLEM WINDOWS

Either because of their unusual shape or inaccessibility, some windows cannot easily be fitted with curtains or blinds. Very often, by applying a little ingenuity and thought, these problems can be solved easily.

Windows with a sloping top are often set directly under a sloping ceiling. If this is the case, there are several things you can do. The first, if you are not in direct view, is to paint the frame in a bright color that contrasts with the rest of the room, and leave the window uncovered. Alternatively, if the room is used for sleeping, you can attach a roller blind to the frame. Choose a second contrasting color for the blind and set it inside the horizontal frame to offset both the window and room interior.

If you prefer to have curtains, either hang sheers or a café curtain from the horizontal line of the window – these windows are usually plain vertical casements with angular-shaped panes of glass above. Shutters may also be used – they can be specially cut to shape, or fitted only over the lower rectangular part of the window.

If the ceiling does not slope directly above the window, you could attach a *trompe-l'oeil* pelmet or valance so that it runs straight across the window from the highest point, disguising the sloping angle of the frame. The curtain can then be hung on a horizontal track below. Under these circumstances, you could also hang sheers. They should be hung slightly higher than the highest point of the angle and several widths of fabric will be required.

Pivot windows are often seen in new houses and flats, and appear to have been designed oblivious of any need for curtains or blinds. If the window pivots horizontally, it is possible to use a conventional curtain on a track, so long as the track is extended sufficiently far at either side of the window so that the undrawn curtains hang well clear of the pivot mechanism. Each pivoting frame could also be treated as a separate entity, with a small or sheer curtain hung from coiled wires or narrow rods attached to the top and bottom of the frame. If you use this method make sure that the fabric

Above: Blinds are the most common solution to problem windows – even one with an angle has been successfully covered, using a rod to hold the blind in the corner. Use a tough fabric to avoid wear.

Right: A sharply angled glass

extension is successfully curtained with the aid of two tracks. One is positioned at the peak of the roof, and the other just below the sloping window.

Far right: tracks just inside the skylight reveal hold runners that gather the blind into soft pleats.

used is lightweight with a fairly plain weave, or the final effect could be cluttered and clumsy.

If the window pivots vertically, a sheer curtain can be attached to the pivoting frame itself – also at both top and bottom – to solve the problem of privacy, while a Venetian or pleated blind that retracts neatly into a box-shaped heading might well solve the problem of light.

Corner windows, which meet with little space between, pose another problem. One solution – depending on the amount of space in the corner – would be to have a dummy corner curtain, with two other curtains set at either side of the two windows and drawn back to expose the frame. Although only the two outer curtains would draw, there would be an appearance of symmetry. Alternatively, a corner window seat, with or without a pelmet and valance, could be fitted and covered with the same fabric as the curtains, which

would draw attention away from the problem. The two outer curtains would, in effect, create a frame to both the seat and the window.

Blinds are not a very practical solution to the problem since the two inner edges would probably catch in use, but sheers can work well, again disguising the angularity of the two windows.

Set-together windows If they are very close, these windows should be treated as one large window, and curtained accordingly. A pelmet or valance that runs across both windows can do much to offset any irregularity in either the size of the windows or the area of wall surrounding them. Sheers can be used to good effect, with or without main curtains, but blinds are best coordinated with curtains – perhaps formal dress curtains – in order to emphasize the regularity of the two windows.

UNDRESSED WINDOWS

Windows need not be covered uniformly for the sake of order or convention. Only one window here is curtained, while the other, more decorative ones are boldly left unadorned.

Arched windows create the focal point for a stylish kitchen/dining room, and are wisely left bare, their shutters just painted with dark green paint to match their frames.

Windows have an aesthetic as well as a practical role to play; many are much better left uncovered so that their proportions can be fully appreciated. Look at your windows and see which, if any, would be better left alone.

Many windows that are not beautifully proportioned or detailed often benefit by being thrown into the limelight. There are several ways of bringing out a window, turning it into a positive addition to the room. Window frames can be painted using deeper tones or contrasting colors in the recesses. They can also be edged with a decorative border, or you can stencil a design around them. Where there are deep windowsills, use them for displaying books, plants or interesting bits and pieces.

Architectural windows is a term which loosely encompasses windows which are more of an architectural indulgence than a necessity. They should be left unadorned as a design feature.

Stained glass windows are obvious examples of those that require no covering. There are many fine examples of both nineteenth- and twentieth-century stained glass and they are generally being appreciated again after being disliked for some years. Along with delicate etched or painted glass, these windows should be treated as a decorative focal point. If these panels are not in a window that gets a lot of sun, it can be worth moving them to a lighter spot.

Period windows that were built during the great architectural eras – particularly those of the eighteenth century – should be regarded critically before being covered. Many still retain their original shutters, and these with their deep, heavily molded frames often need only the correct paint treatment for them to dominate the room.

Staircase If you can, try to avoid covering any window on the stairs unless you have to. Too often stairs are narrow, steep and dark, and the window plays an essential part in safety and practicality.

CURTAINS

Right: Consider the quality of light and the style of furnishing you have when choosing curtains. A bright corridor with lovely antiques is best served by muslin tied loosely on rods.

In every home there are some rooms and some windows where only curtains will do – you may love blinds to distraction, but there are times when they are just not the right treatment for the situation.

Curtains have a multiplicity of uses, both practical and decorative, and it is important that yours fill as many of those uses as possible. They should, for example, keep out cold, keep in heat and shut out light when necessary. They should also set the scene for the room and your possessions.

Curtains not only affect the appearance of the windows they cover but also alter our perception of the room as a whole. Floor-length curtains with a pelmet and valance will stress the vertical, sill-length ones – extended beyond the window – will emphasize the horizontal. Softly draped curtains, swagged and swept back with ties, will disguise hard angles, while narrow plain curtains used with a roller blind will give the window a clean, sharp look. Bright colors will draw attention to themselves, while pale shades and simple designs will turn the eye away.

Curtains can be bought, ready made, in many standard sizes and designs from most large department stores. They pick their best-selling fabric designs, and a few perennial favorites such as velvet, and have them made up into curtains of widths and lengths which will fit most average-size windows. So if your windows are relatively normal, these curtains could well be a good idea.

Curtains can also be made by professional curtain-makers. At curtain-making's simplest level, there are shops and individuals who will simply follow your measurements and place your chosen material back-to-back with its lining, seam them both, turn them right way around, sew on a heading tape and then hem them. A process which is known, not surprisingly, as bagging.

And then there are the true professional curtain-makers who come to you, and stand by your window, taking measurement after measurement. To use these craftsmen is a course of action that may seem expensive, not to say extravagant, but which for many people is justified by the high standard of expertise and the time saved. The best curtain-makers make all the headings by hand. The curtains are fully lined and interlined, and weighted to hang properly, and then finished off by hand. They are then hung and adjusted until absolutely perfect. If you are thinking of using a very expensive fabric, it is often worth finding out how much a professional would charge you – they usually charge by the drop (or length). It is then fairly easy to calculate and compare the prices based on the number of drops you expect your curtains to have. As with all craftsmen, the best way to choose a professional curtain-maker is to see examples of their work, ideally *in situ.*

Then, of course, you can make the curtains yourself. This is really not a difficult task, provided you take time to measure accurately at the beginning, and take care with each step. The job itself has been made much easier and more enjoyable nowadays thanks to the ready availability of various heading tapes and the wide range of tracks and decorative poles, plus every refinement a curtain-maker could want. The money to be saved by making them yourself is enormous, and you will have the endless satisfaction of knowing that it was all your own work. If you do decide to make them yourself, don't be daunted by all those yards of uncut material lying on the floor – they will soon be tamed into stylish window dressings. Also, when making them yourself it is worth spending just that little bit more time and energy on lining and interlining them whenever necessary. A well-made pair of curtains should last a lifetime, fabric willing, and it doesn't take much more time to make them well than to make them badly.

If you are making them for the first time, go for simplicity, either a plain fabric or a small print or stripe which can be matched easily. Remember, curtains don't have to be elaborate. A simple, clear color, unadorned by tie-backs or pelmets, etc., can look just as good, if well made, as the most elaborately embellished scene stealer.

Not all windows come undressed, however, many windows come along with inherited curtains that could most kindly be described as adequate. Cheer them up by adding a few touches here or there: decorative tie-backs, borders, a pelmet or valance, or braids.

FABRIC TYPES

Fabrics

BROCADE Medium-weight fabric with a woven-in raised design. The design can be contrasting or self-colored.

BRODERIE ANGLAISE Machine-made embroidered fabric.

CALICO Firm, bleached or unbleached cotton.

CHINTZ Firm, medium-weight cotton, printed with floral or bird designs and treated with a glaze finish.

COTTON Plain-woven fabric, can be glazed. The most commonly used fabric in home furnishings.

COTTON LINING Plain-woven cotton that comes in a range of colors as well as buff and white.

DAMASK Plain-colored jacquard-woven fabric.

DOMETTE Soft, open-weave fabric used as interlining.

GINGHAM Lightweight, distinctively checked or striped cotton or cotton mix.

LACE Open-weave, intricately patterned fabric. Can be made from cotton or synthetic fibers.

LAWN Lightweight, soft, fine-woven fabric.

LINEN Fabric made from strong fiber, can be bought in a variety of weights and weaves.

MOIRÉ Fabric with a crossways rib and watermarking effect.

MUSLIN Plain-woven, medium- to lightweight cotton.

NET Open, mesh fabric, either in cotton or man-made fibers.

NYLON Strong synthetic fiber, often blended and used for shower curtains.

PLASTIC Synthetic unbacked fabric, commonly used for shower curtains.

REFLECTIVE LINING Lining fabric coated on one side with metallic particles to reflect heat and light.

SATEEN Similar to satin, but usually cotton.

SATIN Lustrous fabric made in different weights and fibers.

SEERSUCKER Lightweight fabric, treated to produce a crinkled surface. Usually made of cotton.

SILK Natural, luxurious fabric, found in many different weights and weaves.

VELVET Pile fabric either cotton or cotton mix.

VELVETEEN Short-pile cotton fabric similar to velvet.

VOILE Soft, sheer, plain-weave fabric.

WOOL Natural fiber, usually blended with other fibers.

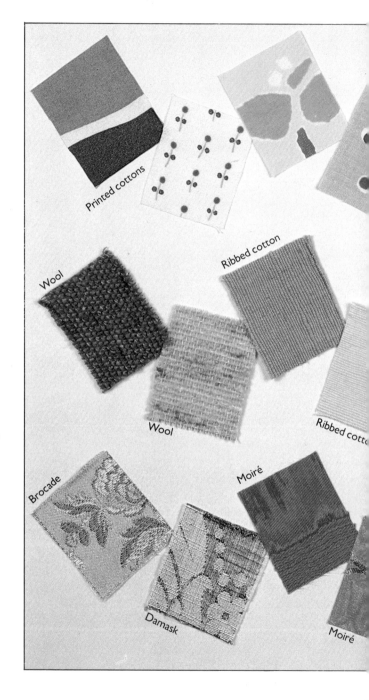

Printed cottons

Wool

Ribbed cotton

Wool

Ribbed cotton

Brocade

Moiré

Damask

Moiré

Calico

Gingham

Seersucker

Lawn

Lace

Net

Velvet

Silk

Velvet

en

Glazed cotton

Satin

Chintz

Sateen

A selection from the vast range of
fabrics which can be used for curtains
and blinds – simple, jolly cottons
through slubby wools, lace and net
to luxurious silks and velvets.

CALCULATING FABRIC AMOUNT

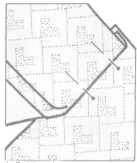

When cutting out the fabric, spread the fabric out on a large flat surface and cut straight across the width using large, sharp scissors. On fabrics with all-over patterns, straighten the edge, then measure and cut each length. With large print fabrics, follow the design lines when cutting out each piece. To find the straight edge on even-weave fabrics, pull out a thread and cut along the gap.

When buying curtain fabric, it is important to have calculated exactly how much you will need in advance. Apart from other considerations, bolts of the same fabric may have slight variations of pattern or color and, if it were necessary to buy more fabric, there could well be a distinct difference in the finished curtains which is often only noticeable when they are being hung.

The length and fullness of a curtain are the first things to be taken into account. As a rule, the length should fall either to the sill, radiator or to the floor. If you choose floor length, decide whether the curtains are to sit just above the floor, touch it, or overflow on to it.

The next step is to choose the style of heading, and this, with your chosen length, will determine the total amount of fabric needed. Some headings require a large amount of fabric while others use much less. A pencil-pleated heading, for example, needs two and a quarter to two and a half times the length of the curtain track, while a simple, gathered heading needs only one and a half to two times the track length (*see page 43*).

Before measuring the window area, either mark the position or put up the pole or track from which the curtains will hang, as this will obviously affect their finished length. Work out whether your track or pole is to be fixed inside or outside the window frame, or extended beyond the frame on both sides. A curtain pole with decorative finials is always supported on brackets outside the window frame.

Although most curtain fabrics are a fairly standard width of 48 inches, there are variations, particularly with imported fabrics, so in calculating the amounts needed, always double check the width of the fabric you plan to use.

Once you have established the track, or pole, and chosen the style of heading, measure the length from the correct position at the top edge to the bottom and add 8 inches for hem and heading. For the width, multiply the length of the track by the required fullness for the style of heading plus 4 to 6 inches for the side turnings, then divide by the width of your chosen fabric – usually 48 inches – and round up this figure to the nearest full number to give the number of

1. Fold under seam allowance and pin over seam allowance of adjoining piece.

2. Stitch across the join between the two fabrics and run through the flat fabric.

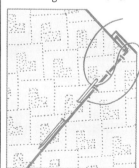

3. Take the needle back across join and through folded fabric. Continue.

Measuring for curtains

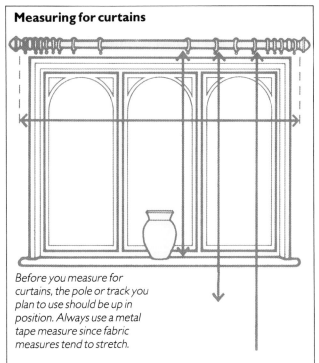

Before you measure for curtains, the pole or track you plan to use should be up in position. Always use a metal tape measure since fabric measures tend to stretch.

- Measure the length from the track or pole to the desired height: to the sill, to the top of a radiator below the sill or to the floor. Then add allowances for hem and heading.

- For the width, multiply the track or pole length by the required fullness of the desired heading tape.

- Divide this measurement by the fabric width, rounding up the figure to the nearest full number for the number of fabric widths per curtain.

- Multiply the curtain length by the number of fabric widths for the amount of fabric needed.

- The amount of lining required will be the same as the amount of curtain fabric – but remember to deduct any extra that might have been required to match up patterns.

standard fabric widths needed. Half fabric widths can be used in curtain making when the amount of fabric needed is slightly over a full number. Position half widths on the outside edge of the curtain. Multiply the curtain length by the total number of fabric widths to get the amount of fabric needed.

It is sometimes tempting to try and save on fabric, especially when you see how many widths you will need, but this is always a false economy. The difference between good- and cheap-looking curtains has a lot to do with the fullness of fabric. If in doubt, it is always better to err on the side of having too much rather than too little.

Unless a washable fabric has been fully pre-shrunk it is always necessary to allow for shrinkage. This is usually 3-4 per cent on a curtain which is less than 2 yards long, and the normal hem allowance will accommodate this.

If you are using fabrics with a distinct pattern, it is essential, if you plan on joining together more than one width of fabric in a curtain, to make sure that the patterns match horizontally at the seams. This is done by allowing extra fabric so that the pattern repeats can be adjusted to match. Most assistants at curtain fabric counters are adept at calculating the quantity required (if they have the basic window measurement), but, as a rough guide, measure the height of the pattern repeat and add that measurement to the length of each width after the first one, so that the pattern can be matched exactly to the adjacent width.

This is done by first ladder-stitching the lengths together from the right side with the pattern matching exactly – see steps left; then fold the fabric lengths with right sides together and machine-stitch together on the wrong side and complete with the appropriate seam.

For the amount of lining fabric needed, calculate as for the main fabric even though the lining hem is slightly higher than that of the curtain fabrics. If extra curtain fabric is needed for matching patterns, remember to deduct this from the amount of lining fabric required. Generally, lining fabrics are also 48 inches wide, but they are sometimes available in a limited range of wider widths and using these can, in some cases, be cheaper.

HEADINGS

If you plan to have curtains without elaborate valances or pelmets, then the curtain heading itself will become an important feature. The choice of heading has as much to do with the length and proportion of the curtain as it does with personal taste.

Cased headings

Curtains such as café curtains, short nets and sheers and some long curtains – provided they are lightweight and unlined – can be attached with a simple sewn channel, made by turning over the top of the curtain and machine-sewing two rows of stitching to form a channel, through which a rod or expanding wire can be slotted. The gathered fabric makes a small frill, or heading, at the top.

For the amount of fullness, allow about one and a half times the length of the rod. For the depth, measure from the top of the rod to the required curtain length plus 4 inches for the hem and the correct heading allowance. The heading is usually ½ to ¾ inches and the casing ½ inch, which may have to be adjusted to fit your method of fixing so decide on the method and then add the correct allowance, remembering to allow for a double width casing.

Heading tapes

These are narrow strips of strong fabric that can be bought by the metre (yard) in a variety of types and sizes. They are available in white and natural in both cotton and synthetic fibres. For example, lightweight synthetic tapes should be used for synthetic fabrics, sheers and nets. The tapes usually have two or more cords running through the middle and when they are pulled up together form a gathered or pleated heading, depending on the style used. They also have slots for

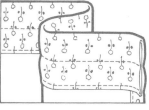

Cased heading

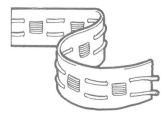

Standard heading tape

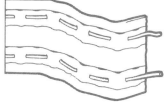

Pencil-pleat tape

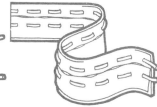

Detachable-lining tape

Attaching standard tape

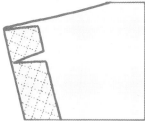

1. Snip into hem along fold line, to within ¼ inch of outer edge. Match edges; fold over.

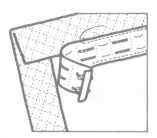

2. At one end of tape, knot cords on wrong side. Turn under tape end and sew.

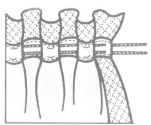

3. At opposite end of tape, pull out cords from the front and gather up curtain.

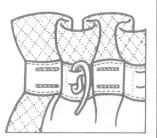

4. Then thread the hooks through the tape, evenly spaced across the curtain.

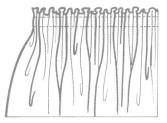

Standard *One and a half to two times track length of fabric is needed.*

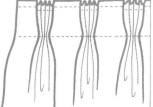

Cluster *Required fullness is two times the track length of fabric.*

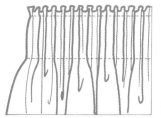

Pencil *Fullness required is two and a quarter to two and a half times.*

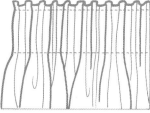

Spaced pencil pleats *Two and a quarter times the track length in fabric is required.*

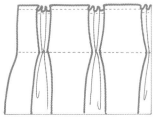

Triple pleats *are either straight or fanned. Two times the track length is needed.*

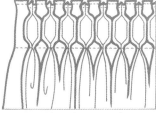

Decorative, *for example smocking. Two times the track length is needed.*

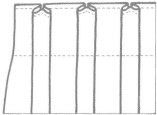

Box *Semi-formal in appearance, these pleats are evenly spaced. Two and a half times the track length of fabric is needed.*

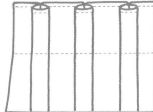

Cartridge *Softly rounded pleats. Two to two and a half times the track length of fabric is needed.*

the hooks, which attach the tape to the curtain runners on the track. The deeper tapes have more than one row of slots so that the height of the curtain above the track can be adjusted by inserting the hooks in either row of slots. Special tapes are also available for detachable linings to be used with any curtain heading tape.

With pairs of curtains, it is important that the style of heading should match in the middle where they butt together – particularly on triple and cartridge-pleat tapes where there is a wide space between each group of pleats. This does not apply if you have an overlap arm on the track. To match the heading, always begin by placing the tape to the curtain edge that will fall in the middle of the track, starting in the center of a pleat group.

STANDARD PLEATS The tapes for standard pleats form a simple gathered heading suitable for all weights of fabric. Its plain, shallow heading is usually covered by a pelmet or valance. It is particularly useful for small unlined curtians.

CLUSTER PLEATS This gives a fairly shallow heading of evenly spaced pleats suitable for all fabric weights.

PENCIL PLEATS This tape makes a deeper, more formal heading suitable for all types of unlined curtains, lined cotton and sheers and some medium-weight fabrics for use with a track or pole. Spaced pencil-pleat tape is ideal for heavier fabrics. Make sure the gathers are evenly distributed.

TRIPLE PLEATS Either straight or fanned, these form a deep, stiffened heading suitable for formal lined curtains of all lengths for use on a track or pole. They are ideal for all types of cottons, and medium- to heavyweight fabrics.

CARTRIDGE PLEATS These softly rounded and distinctly formal pleats are suitable for all types of curtain – especially for heavier, lined, floor-length curtains.

DECORATIVE HEADINGS These tapes give a crisp decorative appearance and can be used on short or long curtains – lined or unlined – using cotton, medium-weight or sheer fabrics.

BOX PLEATS These give a semi-formal appearance and can be used for all types of curtains and sheers hung from a track or pole. They are especially good for thicker, lined curtains.

MAKING CURTAINS

Making unlined curtains

Apart from those curtains made from self-edged nets and sheer fabrics, the technique for making an unlined curtain is basic to making any other type.

Begin by joining the fabric widths together using ⅝ inch flat fell seams, having first removed or snipped into the selvedges. Turn over 1 inch double turnings on the side edges and a 3 inch double hem on the bottom edge, and press to the wrong side.

Miter the bottom corners. After basting and slip-stitching the miter, continue to slip-stitch around the sides and hem using a matching-colored sewing thread, picking up only one or two threads of flat fabric with each stitch. Enclose weights in the hem, if needed (see page 47), and finish the top edge with your chosen heading (see page 42).

MITERING A CORNER With the curtain wrong side up, and the side and bottom turnings pressed in place, mark the turnings at the outer edge with pins. Unfold the corner to leave single turnings and then fold the fabric diagonally from pin to pin. Refold the side turning and the hem, baste and slip-stitch the miter together working from the outer corner to the inside edge.

Unlined curtains

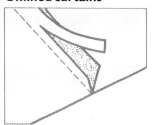 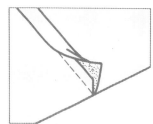 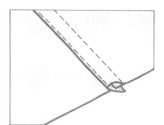 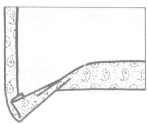

1. To join widths place fabric right sides together; machine. Trim one allowance in half.

2. Fold wider seam allowance over narrower seam allowance; press against fabric.

3. To enclose and neaten the raw edges stitch down seam again, close to fold edge.

4. Turn in 1 inch double turnings on side edges and a double 3 inch hem.

Loose-lined curtains

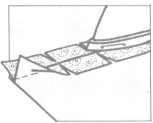 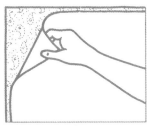 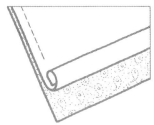 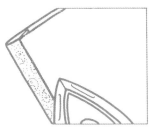

1. After stitching widths together snip into the seam allowance and press open.

2. Place lining and fabric with right sides together, matching side edges.

3. Stitch down sides to within 6 inches of hem. Turn up a double 1 inch lining hem.

4. Matching centers press curtain, so side seams lie ¾ inch in from outer edges.

Making lined curtains

Unless the curtains are semi-sheer and intended to filter light, use a lining. It will protect the curtain fabric from sunlight – giving it extra life – and reduce heat loss and noise.

Loose-lining The side edges are stitched together, the top edges treated as one, and the bottom hems stitched separately. First, calculate the amount of fabric needed; it should be 1¾ inches narrower than the finished curtain.

Join the main fabric and lining widths, using ⅝ inch flat seams. Clip into the selvedges, and raw edges, every 4 to 6 inches, and press them open. With right sides together, place the lining to the main fabric and, taking ⅝ inch seams, machine-stitch the sides to within 6 inches of lining edge. Clip the seams. Turn up a double 1 inch hem on the lining, miter the corners and slip-stitch to close. Machine-stitch the hem. Turn the curtain right side out, match the centers of both fabrics and press the side edges. Turn up a double 2 inches hem on main fabric; miter and finish as for unlined curtains. Slip-stitch the rest of the lining to side edges.

Turn down top edge, cutting and turning in the corners at a slight angle. Add your chosen heading tape.

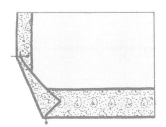 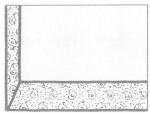 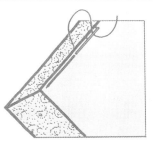 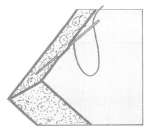

5. Mark turnings with pins. Unfold corner then fold corner diagonally through both pins.

6. Refold in side and hem edges, so miter is formed across the corner; slip-stitch.

7. Slip-stitch down side edges, just picking up one or two stitches of flat fabric.

8. Slide the needle through the folded hem edge and bring out ready for the next stitch.

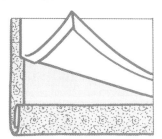  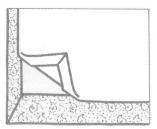 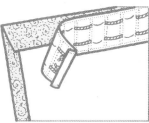

5. Turn up a double 2 inches hem on the bottom edge of the main fabric.

6. Miter the corner of the main fabric in the same way as for unlined curtains.

7. Slip-stitch the remainder of the side seam down to the lining hem edge.

8. Turn down the top edges at an angle (if necessary). Attach heading tape.

Right: Curtains made using professional techniques are both long-lasting and opulent looking: two headings, pencil and pinch, are used here, with elaborate plaited tie-backs.

Lock-stitched lining The technique of lock-stitching the lining and main fabric together is used by professional curtain-makers and gives a better finish to the hang of the curtain. It is worked in vertical rows across the curtain width and involves lightly catching the lining to the curtain fabric with large loose stitches.

First, estimate the amount of curtain fabric needed, and allow the same amount of lining minus allowances all round. With the main fabric right side down, press in 2 inch single turnings on the side edges, and a 6 inch single turning on the hem. Miter the corners as for unlined curtains, using single turnings only. Slip-stitch the miter together. Herringbone-stitch down both side edges and across the hem, picking up only one or two threads of the main fabric. Turn in and press ¾ inch on side edges and a 2 inch hem on the lining mitering and stitch the corners in the same way.

Place the curtain fabric right side down on a flat surface, and then the lining on top, right side up. Smooth flat and pin down the center. Fold half the curtain fabric back and lock-stitch the lining to the main fabric from the top edge to just above hem edge and taking long, loose stitches. Work more rows of lock-stitch about 16 inches apart across the curtain width working from the center outward both ways, with rows of stitching beginning at the top and working towards the hem.

Smooth the lining in place and slip-stitch to the side edges and hem, covering the raw edges of the main fabric. Fold over the top edge of the curtain fabric and lining. On heavy fabrics, miter and slip-stitch the corners. Baste the turning and apply your chosen heading.

Interlining will undoubtedly add a professional quality to your curtains. A soft layer of fabric stitched between the curtain fabric and lining will make them hang in beautiful rounded folds as well as provide an effective insulation against cold drafts and protect expensive curtain fabric from dust and strong sunlight. With interlined curtains, it is usual to lock-stitch the interlining to the fabric, then add the lining in the same way as for lock-stitch linings.

Lock-stitch lining

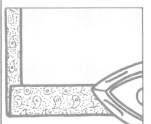

1. Turn in 2 inch single side turnings and 6 inch hem at the base edge and press.

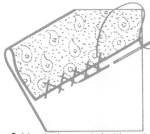

2. Herringbone stitch side and hem edges, only taking one or two threads of fabric.

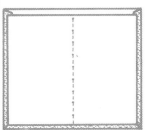

3. Place lining over curtain fabric, wrong sides facing, and pin together down the center.

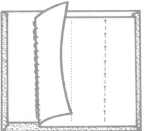

4. Work rows of vertical lock-stitching from the center outwards across the curtain.

5. Make long loose lock-stitches in a thread that matches the fabric, picking up only one or two threads.

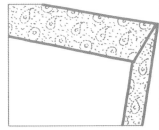

6. On heavier fabrics, miter the top corners of the curtain before adding the heading tape to the top folded edge.

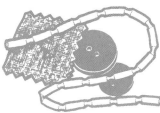

Two types of curtain weight: discs with two central holes are stitched in place like a button, or enclosed inside a fabric bag. Alternatively, fabric-covered weights, they come in a continuous length which is stitched down at intervals along the hemline.

Calculate the amount of curtain fabric and lining needed as for lock-stitched lining. You will need the same amount of interlining as the finished flat curtain. Widths of interlining should be overlapped by about ⅜ inch and then herringbone-stitched together.

It should then be spread on a flat surface (floor if needed) and the curtain fabric placed on top, right side up, smoothed flat and pinned down the center. Half the curtain fabric is folded back and lock-stitched as for lock-stitched lining. This is repeated every 16 inches across the curtain width. Baste around the outside edges through both layers.

Turn the fabrics over and, with the interlining on top, make single turnings on the side edges and hem, and stitch as for lock-stitched lining. Apply the lining and heading in the same way. When lock-stitching the lining, avoid stitching over the same rows made when lock-stitching the interlining.

Interlining

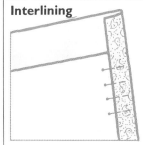

1. Overlap the edges of the interlining by ⅜ inch and herringbone stitch.

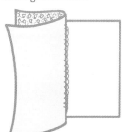

2. Fold back the curtain fabric and lock-stitch to the interlining down the center.

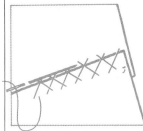

3. Turn in side edges, and complete in the same way as for lock-stitched lining.

SHEERS

Sheer curtains, used mainly to provide privacy or to hide a dull view, can be plainly draped, decoratively frilled or swathed while still letting in pleasantly diffused daylight. Depending on your interior scheme, choose either crisp, floral lace or reproduction Victorian panels for a traditional effect, or semi-sheer with dramatic geometric patterns, or color-flecked voiles for a modern look.

Sheer, semi-sheer and fine net fabrics can be bought by the yard in standard widths between 36 and 120 inches from an enormous variety of patterns, textures and fibres mostly in pure white and natural colors, with some pastel semi-sheers; the synthetic varieties are mostly drip-dry, shrinkproof and resistant to sunlight. Sheer curtains can also be bought as "long" and "short nets" requiring very little finishing. Long nets, with decorative selvedges, come in several widths and are sold by the length required, while short nets, with

decorative hems, come in standard depths and are sold by the width needed.

When making curtains, allow adequate fullness of two to three times the track length. As so many widths of sheer fabrics are available, seams are not often necessary. Where two widths do have to be used the selvedges can hang together, concealed in the fullness of the curtain. If a seam is necessary, stitch together with narrow flat fell seams.

For formal window dressing, where sheers are used to provide privacy, they are best kept simple and hung close to the window with formal headed curtains at each side. The sheer might be self-patterned or color-coordinated to the dress curtains.

A classic window treatment for tall windows using a sheer simply as a foil against the light is to hang a simple off-white curtain from a plain wooden pole. The width should be three times the pole length for fullness and allow the curtain to flow onto the floor. The hem should be weighted so the drifting mass of fabric can be arranged neatly, and the formal heading attached by rings. Alternatively, you can create a rather grand effect with floor-length sheers by draping more of the same fabric over the pole into loosely shaped swags seamed from behind with judiciously placed staples or pushpins.

Half, café or tiered curtains – often essential for privacy – can be very pretty and give the opportunity to use heavier figured lace or those sheers with decorative lower borders. All can hang quite simply from cased headings or, as an attractive alternative, from colored ribbons tied over a pole.

Reproduction Victorian lace panels – showing a picture rather than a repeat design – are ideally suited to French windows, especially those in older houses. The panels, with wires slotted through cased headings, are fitted neatly over each window, offering both privacy and easy access to the doors which are not impeded by the coverings.

Tied-back crossover nets or sheers can be used to correct the proportion of a window or to conceal an unattractive view. They make a pretty window treatment for bedrooms, and can be frilled and flamboyant or plainly draped depending on your choice.

Sheer and semi-sheer fabrics offer many more possibilities than their image of the net-twitching old lady at the window would suggest.

Far left: A stylish dotted voile combines well with a turn-of-the-century fabric design for a romantic little breakfast room.

Left: Pleated muslin carefully pinned to a wood frame in an arched window enhances the shape and brings a dramatic softness to an otherwise cool and restrained room.

HANGING CURTAINS

The unseen parts of curtain hanging are the most important of all – no matter how well a curtain is made, the effect will be ruined if it is hanging like a drunken sailor from the track.

Tracks

It is essential to decide at the beginning exactly how you want your curtains to be attached. Tracks can be fixed either to the ceiling or to the window frame – to the width of the frame, or extended beyond and attached to the wall. You should also decide whether or not to have a pelmet or valance to cover the track. If so, the track itself need not be elaborate. A soft valance usually needs a second track which is either clipped to the curtain track or fixed on extended brackets outside it.

If you decide to have a track without a pelmet or valance, then the track should be as unobtrusive as possible. There are several types available in plain and colored plastic – produced in a fairly limited range of colors.

Metal tracks are on the whole sturdier – and more expensive. They are recommended for heavier curtains, which need a lot of support.

Tracks for bow and bay windows should be sufficiently pliable for them to be bent accurately to shape. As with other windows, you may prefer your curtains to overlap in the middle of the window. In that case, the extended track should also be cut and bent to fit. Both tracks should overlap each other by up to 6 inches.

Poles

These are available in several different styles and decorative finishes made from wood, brass and other metals. Wooden poles can be mitered to fit around bay windows and some metal poles are adjustable. Many of them are accurate reproductions of antique poles – often with beautiful decorative finials. They can be bought in standard and made-to-measure lengths, complete with the appropriate rings and brackets, with or without cords, and in various colors.

Where uncorded poles are used, especially with heavier fabrics, it is best to buy draw rods. These hang from behind, attached to the runners close to the heading edges.

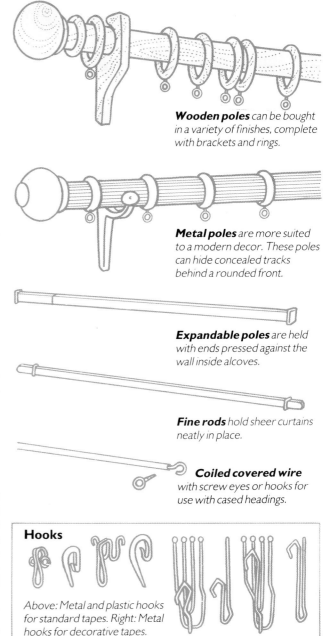

Wooden poles can be bought in a variety of finishes, complete with brackets and rings.

Metal poles are more suited to a modern decor. These poles can hide concealed tracks behind a rounded front.

Expandable poles are held with ends pressed against the wall inside alcoves.

Fine rods hold sheer curtains neatly in place.

Coiled covered wire with screw eyes or hooks for use with cased headings.

Hooks

Above: Metal and plastic hooks for standard tapes. Right: Metal hooks for decorative tapes.

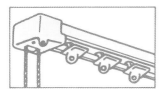

Ceiling-mounted *tracks are a useful alternative system.*

Wall-mounted *track with an overlap arm.*

Valance rail *clips onto the front of the main track.*

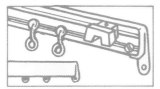

Concealed *standard track in white plastic.*

Rods

For lightweight curtains such as nets, sheers and café curtains, you can buy thin metal rods and coiled wires – for slotting through a cased heading – which are supported by small hooks and screw eyes. These metal rods come either in chrome, brass or with a white plastic finish.

Adjustable rods are also available in either a plastic or brass finish. The plastic type has a spring mechanism which allows it to fit a variable space, and is fitted inside the window reveal. The other kind works like a telescope at one end and is fixed either inside or outside the window with brackets.

Hooks

These come in many different shapes and sizes, in both plastic and metal finishes. Plastic hooks are usually sold in conjunction with plastic runners specifically designed for plastic tracks. For best results, a hook should be inserted at each end of the curtain and about every 3 inches in between.

Metal hooks made from brass or aluminum are much stronger and should always be used on heavier fabrics. They include the standard curtain hook and hooks for the drawstring heading tapes, as well as pronged hooks for slotted curtain tapes. These hooks are sold separately and in two sizes – for hanging higher or lower on the track or pole – so make sure you have the right hooks.

New curtain poles are sold with fittings attached into which a standard hook is fitted. Metal hooks are used on hand-stitched headings, where they are stitched behind the pleats.

Runners

Runners are designed to glide easily along the pole or track and have loops at the bottom for holding the hooks attached to the curtain. They are usually made to suit a particular track and include the traditional rings in brass, wood or plastic for rods and poles, and plastic- or brass-finished runners that hang from specially shaped tracks either from the lower edge or slot into the back of the track. Most runners have the hook suspended in such a way that, when the curtains are hung, both the track and runners are hidden. One type of runner combines a second loop to hold the hooks on the lining at the same time. Nowadays, combined hooks and runners are sold with some tracks.

The runner on the outer end of the track – usually called an end-stop – is anchored to the track and stops the curtain from sliding off, and the outer hook is slotted into the runner on the outer edge of the track.

Cord pulls

Whether you have plastic or metal tracks, pelmets, or valances, if your track does not have integral cord pulls, it is worth thinking of adding a cording set. These cords are specially fitted so that the curtains can be opened and closed simply by pulling an extension of the cord fitted to one side of the window, thus preventing wear to the curtain edge by constant pulling. One set of cords, for example, can also be arranged to operate sets of curtains on double windows, if they have a combined track.

Dressing the curtains

After hanging curtains – especially the heavier floor-length ones – the folds and pleats need to be "set" so that they hang evenly from heading to floor.

Open the curtains to the draw-back position and straighten each fold and pleat. On cartridge-pleated curtains, each of the pleats can be lightly stuffed to hold their rounded shape – use tissue paper, or a soft tissue. When all the folds are even, tie soft ribbon or cord around the curtain at the top and bottom. Leave for about three days for the folds to set.

ACCESSORIES

Cords and ropes

For a period, classic look, use cords or passamenterie. These can be bought already knotted, with or without tassels. They come in different thicknesses and fibers, including metallic threads, and in a full range of colors and they can occasionally be dyed to order.

Borders and trims

Some manufacturers of cords also make matching colored borders and trims – in furnishing weights – in a wide variety of designs. They are used often for edging plain or patterned floor-length curtains, pelmets and valances, and can also be applied to other soft furnishings, such as sofas and chairs.

Tie-backs

Adding a touch of prettiness or formality to many curtain types, tie-backs are essentially a useful way of keeping the curtain clear of the window in order to let in as much light as possible. Choose them with care. Before deciding, it is a good plan to spend time experimenting with different ideas. First, draw the curtains away from the window and tie them loosely with a length of string. Move the string into different positions to see which is best. Stand back so that you can see how well the curtains fall.

Tie-backs can be plain or decorative bands of fabric which are held in place by small rings attached to the ends and a hook fixed to the window frame. Shaped tie-backs are usually stiffened with interfacing or buckram and look parti-

Making tie-backs

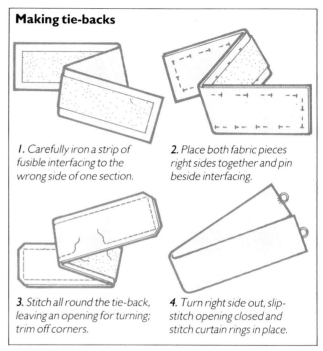

1. Carefully iron a strip of fusible interfacing to the wrong side of one section.

2. Place both fabric pieces right sides together and pin beside interfacing.

3. Stitch all round the tie-back, leaving an opening for turning; trim off corners.

4. Turn right side out, slip-stitch opening closed and stitch curtain rings in place.

cularly good with an elaborate pelmet. They are quite easy to make provided you use a paper pattern. Tie-backs can be made from matching or contrasting colored fabrics or different-patterned fabrics. The edges can be piped, bound or trimmed with braid.

Some of the most successful and original tie-backs may be nothing more than a length of self fabric tied in a simple bow, or pieces of fabric that would be hard to display elsewhere. A pretty silk scarf tie-back, for example, made by tying the fabric in a loose bow or knot, or a false bow tie, made by using

Tie-backs look good with shaped edges, frills and bows.

Passamenterie with tasselled ends are quick and easy to use.

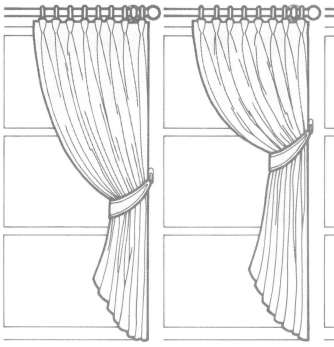

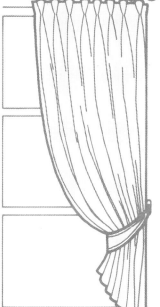

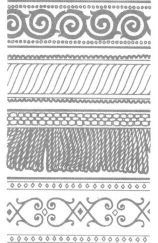

Left: Altering the position of the tie-back round the curtain will dramatically change the look of the curtain and the window.
Below: You can add braids and fringes to plain tie-backs.

the standard tie-back shape with a ready-made bow attached to it, could look good. Plaited tie-backs can look effective, especially in colors picked up from the curtain fabric.

To make a simple tie-back, first measure the required curtain fullness. For each tie-back, cut out two pieces of fabric to this measurement by 4 inches deep (this average depth can be adjusted to curtain proportion) plus an extra ⅝ inch all round, and one piece of iron-on interfacing cut to the finished measurement. Press the interfacing to the wrong side of one section. Baste both sections right sides together and machine

stitch around leaving a 4 inches opening in one side. Trim corners, turn through to right side, press and slip-stitch opening. Attach a curtain ring to each end; just overlap the outer edge and blanket-stitch in place.

For formal window dressing when a pelmet, valance or swags and tails are used, coordinating tie-backs are traditionally used; match up decorative braids.

Reproduction brass rosettes and round-end tie-backs can be bought in several different shapes and sizes, and suit a severe curtain.

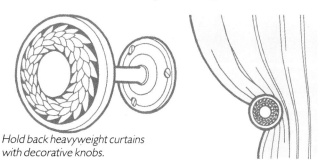

Hold back heavyweight curtains with decorative knobs.

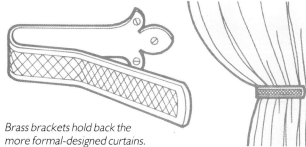

Brass brackets hold back the more formal-designed curtains.

PELMETS AND VALANCES

Pelmets and valances give a decorative and formal finish to the tops of curtains and at the same time hide the curtain heading and track from view. They can be used to create a dramatic effect and to alter the proportion of a window. The pelmet or valance, for example, can be fixed higher than usual to make the window appear taller, or extended at the sides to make it appear wider. Although they are often made from the same fabric as the curtains, they need not match.

Pelmets

Pelmets can be plain wooden boards with either an upholstered, stained or painted finish, or they can be made from stiffened fabric and attached to a pelmet board in the traditional way. The lower edge in each case can be straight or decoratively cut to suit the style of the curtains and general decor of the room.

Before calculating the amount of fabric needed for a pelmet, make sure that the curtain track and pelmet board are fixed in the correct place. The pelmet board should be attached to the wall – usually about 2 to 3 inches above the frame, but this can be varied to suit individual needs.

THE PELMET BOARD should be cut from plywood about 4 inches deep by ½ inch, and project at least 2 to 3 inches at each end of the track, so that the pelmet does not interfere either with the curtain track or the smooth running of the curtains. Screw a 4 inch rectangular piece of plywood at right-angles to each end of the board. Attach the board to the wall with small brackets.

Flat pelmets can have a variety of differently shaped edges. Match the decorative edge to the decor and the curtains.

Making a pelmet

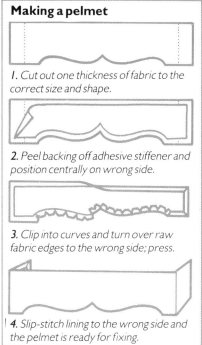

1. Cut out one thickness of fabric to the correct size and shape.

2. Peel backing off adhesive stiffener and position centrally on wrong side.

3. Clip into curves and turn over raw fabric edges to the wrong side; press.

4. Slip-stitch lining to the wrong side and the pelmet is ready for fixing.

Soft, fabric valances should enhance and tone with the curtains hanging beneath them. Use a matching or contrasting fabric.

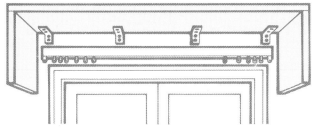

Position pelmet board 2 to 3 inches above and beyond frame.

THE PELMET For the length of fabric needed, measure around the track from wall to wall, and then make a paper pattern of the pelmet shape. Measure the depth – this can vary between one-sixth and one-tenth of a floor-length curtain – and add 1¼ inches all round for turnings. Cut the pelmet stiffener to the finished size, and the lining ⅝ inch larger all round than the stiffener.

Cut out the main fabric across the fabric width so that the weave matches that of the curtains. Join any fabric widths to either side of a central fabric width. Peel backing from one side of stiffener and place centrally on the wrong side of the main fabric; press in place. Clip into the curves and miter the corners on the main fabric before folding the turnings to the wrong side. Peel backing from upper side of stiffener; press fabric turnings onto upper side. Fold in and press ⅝ inch turnings to the wrong side of the lining, and miter the corners. With the lining right side up, press in place to upper side of stiffener, pin and slip-stitch it to the main fabric round the outer edge. If preferred, a decorative trim can be applied to the edge of the pelmet using clear fabric adhesive folding the trim into neat miters at each corner. Hide the join under the miter on one side section.

Stick Velcro spots to wrong side of pelmet, along both edges, 3 inches apart. Stick the opposite halves of spots to the pelmet board to correspond. Press pelmet to board.

Valances

Valances give a softer, more informal look than pelmets. They are usually made from unstiffened fabric and sewn in soft gathers, ruffles or pleats, using handmade or commercial heading tapes. The bottom edge may be plain or gathered – made by gathering or pulling up standard heading tape stitched in vertical rows across the valance. The shape of the valance may follow the original line of the window, or it can be curved to fall down either side of the window, in which case make sure that the depth of the curve is in proportion to the height of the window. Most valances are attached either to a pelmet board with tacks or drawing pins, or a valance track with curtain hooks. They can also have cased headings which would be slotted onto a narrow rod which gathers up the fabric at the same time as holding the valance in position.

For a simple valance using a heading tape, first fix the pelmet board or track in place, and then calculate the amount of fabric needed as for curtains – repeating the same heading on the valance as on the curtain. Estimate the depth in the same proportion as for pelmets. It is usual to line simple gathered valances and interline the other pleated varieties. Cut out the fabric and make up the valance like the curtain.

A professional-looking fabric-covered board pelmet.

FABRIC IDEAS

If you have decided to make your own curtains or blinds, you may well want to extend the creative urge and decorate them yourself – a unique expression of your own style. You could, for example, paint them, or, if you have enjoyed the sewing involved, you could use some form of decorative needlework such as appliqué to finish them off.

One of the simplest ways to create the fabric color you want is to use fabric dyes. Cold and hot water dyes are now available in a wide range of colors and, if the manufacturer's instructions are followed closely, the final effect can be stunning. Some of the new dyes can be used in a washing machine which greatly simplifies the process and removes all the messiness that used to be associated with dyeing fabric.

Fabric painting is popular today, and many companies sell ranges of paints that are specially formulated to be used on fabric. These range from those which are applied with a brush to giant felt-tip-type pens. Alternatively, car bodywork spray paints are very effective. It is always best to first test the paint on an inconspicuous corner of your preferred fabric, and to dry clean when necessary, unless the paint manufacturer's instructions recommend hand-washing.

If you are going to paint directly onto the fabric, wash the material first to remove any sizing or other fabric treatment and then iron it well: you need a completely flat surface on which to work. Close-woven fabrics such as cotton work best with paints, but there is no harm in experimenting with different fabric textures and types. If you feel confident with a paintbrush just lightly pencil your design onto the fabric, and then paint on top. Be bold with your designs; after all, if you are going to all the trouble of painting the curtains yourself, it is worth ensuring that the final work of art is noticed.

As an individual form of decoration, stenciling is more popular than ever before. It is a perfect solution for those of us who like fast, instant results, and also for those of us who don't altogether trust our freehand talents. Stencils can be bought from most good paper shops and range from children's sets with behatted donkeys to stylized renditions of the garlands and flowers loved by early-American craftsmen. There are also books of specialist stencil designs, for example

Art Nouveau or Ancient Egyptian, that you can cut yourself. You can also make your own stencils using stiffened and varnished manila board or stencil card; you will also need a sharp craft knife or stencil knife. Mark a design onto the card, using carbon paper, and then cut carefully around it. Whether you have bought, cut-out or made your stencil, it must, when ready to use, be fixed securely to the fabric. Attach it and the fabric to a flat surface so that neither can move. Use a stubby stencil brush and fabric paints or acrylics. Some professional stencilers use spray paints, which give a fine diffused effect when used properly, but they can be difficult for beginners to handle. Do all the sections that use one of the colors first, before changing to the next color.

The traditional way that stencils were used on curtains was as a border, so try using one that you can extend on to the walls or even onto a wooden floor. Take care when you are attempting a border that when you move your stencil along the fabric, it aligns with the previous motif. Before you begin the design it is a good idea to sew or mark with chalk some sort of guideline.

Appliquéing one fabric onto another is one of the oldest forms of decorative fabric arts. When quilt-making was so popular in the eighteenth and nineteenth centuries, appliqué, rather than patchwork, was the more sophisticated form. Chintzes were rare, and exotic, and motifs such as birds, flowers or leaves would be taken from the prized chintz, carefully cut out, padded, sometimes quilted, and sewn onto a plain quilt which was then itself often heavily embroidered. The finished piece of work was a thing of multi-dimensional beauty.

There is no need to follow such an elaborate procedure today, unless you want to (and there are many specialist books telling you exactly how to go about it), but a simple leaf or bunch of flowers can be cut from a patterned chintz and carefully hemmed by machine or hand onto a plain curtain. An unusual and pretty idea would be to use a border of chintz, cut in one piece with just the edges defined, across the bottom of a curtain, with separate flowers randomly placed across the remainder of the curtain.

The wide range of fabric paints which is now available – from pastel shades through vibrant primaries to pearly finishes – offers enormous potential for creating your own designs. Here, leafy stencils and spray paints have been used on plain linen and cotton for blind, curtains and bedcover to achieve a pretty effect, cheaply.

DRAPERIES

A quick, simple and usually stunning idea for windows is to dress them with asymmetrical draperies. Depending upon the fabrics used and the treatments employed, various effects from opulent grandeur through dreamy romance to stunning simplicity can be achieved with the minimum of fuss and bother. Such draperies are rarely designed to be practical, but they are extremely effective ways of enhancing – or sometimes even disguising – your windows.

Far left: An alternative to the labor of curtain-making is to nail a wooden strip over a pleated drape straight onto the window frame. A coordinating sheer provides privacy.

Center: Even less artifice is needed to throw a large creamy drape over a rod set on brass hooks, to create a simple curtain with a sculptural quality ideal for modern rooms.

Below: The pole-and-hook technique has been used to make a bright bed canopy. A sheer curtain on a pole covers the window effectively without attracting attention.

IMAGINATIVE IDEAS

Left: A carefully planned interior uses a striking fabric to cover the wooden shutters and small scatter cushions. Drapes hung from a ceiling-mounted track create an alcove for a mattress, which acts as a sofa by day and a bed by night.

Above: A very simple pine bed has been transformed into a luxurious four-poster using masses of inexpensive cotton, tied to the bars with tapes. Confident use of the fabric for generous folds is the key to the idea's success.

Right: Brass eyelet kits are easy to use to make these attractive flat-hung blinds which are also reversible, with two layers of fabric stitched together. Dowels are driven into drilled holes in the window frame and painted in contrast to the pegs.

BLINDS

Blinds are a relatively inexpensive and practical solution to covering windows – either large, small or problematical. They help keep out noise and, to some extent, drafts, and also control light, although they are not as efficient as curtains at providing insulation and warmth.

Blinds work very well on small windows and in small rooms, where the amount of fabric in a curtain would otherwise be overpowering. They make ideal coverings for alcoves, shelves or cupboards where there is limited space for outward-opening doors. A series of narrow blinds can also work equally well on large expanses of glass or on awkward sloping windows.

Most blinds are operated either by a spring mechanism and roller, or by a linked cording system and pulleys. They can be wall or window mounted.

Ready-made

There are many excellent ready-made blinds available in very wide ranges of size, color and finish, including roller blinds in stiffened spongable fabrics, pleated paper blinds, wooden slatted blinds, vertical louvers, and Venetian blinds in plastic, wood or metal.

Made-to-measure

Many large department stores offer a made-to-measure service for fabric blinds – normally roller, but sometimes Roman, festoon and Austrian as well. Some will make up from the fabric you supply, but there is usually a wide range of fabric from which to choose, including special blind fabric with, for example, a plain body and a simple pattern across the bottom. Alternatively, there are also studios that will screen-print or hand-paint blinds exclusively for you – this could be the opportunity to improve an uninteresting view or to personalize your blinds in an original way.

Roman blinds are an elegant treatment in keeping with the stark formality of this room. A door leading to the balcony is separately covered, to match.

Measuring for blinds

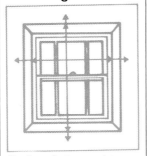

On flat windows, without a recess, measure across the window from one side of the frame to the other. Alternatively, the brackets which hold the blind can be positioned on the wall on either side.

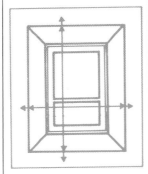

On recessed windows, measure either the width across the inside of the recess or measure across the window outside the recess, then the depth.

Do-it-yourself

Fabric blinds can be quick and easy to make at home. The equipment needed is fairly minimal. Complete roller-blind kits, and the tapes, cords and accessories for Roman, festoon and Austrian blinds, can be bought from most department stores; wooden strips, rods, screws and brackets are available from do-it-yourself suppliers. You will also need standard sewing equipment and a few handyman's tools.

CHOOSING FABRIC Select fabric for blinds with care, avoiding the type of thin, lightweight material that would stretch and sag in the middle, or make untidy edges when rolled up. Equally, heavy fabrics may roll unevenly and bunch up around the roller, or they may put too great a strain on the mountings.

Generally, roller blinds work best with a firm, closely woven fabric such as cotton or cotton/polyester mixes – and these are best in keeping out the light, too. PVC and specially stiffened blind fabric can be bought in wide widths and an excellent choice of fade-resistant colors and patterns, also with spongable finishes and non-fraying edges. These pre-stiffened fabrics do not usually need side hems, but if the blind is to have a lot of use, it is worth turning in a ⅜ inch side hem to prevent fraying.

An alternative is to use spray-on stiffening on other fabrics – even lace can be used as a blind if treated this way. Fabric-stiffening sprays are available in aerosol or liquid form and can be used safely in the home. You will find that most fabrics will shrink slightly when sprayed so allow for this in your basic calculations. To find out how much stiffening a particular fabric will need, test-spray a small piece first in a well-ventilated room and leave to dry. Always follow the manufacturer's instructions as the procedure for different products may vary slightly. Also, spray-stiffened fabrics always need side hems to prevent fraying.

Blinds are hung either flat against the glass inside the window recess or outside the window frame. They can be fixed to the outer molding on a separate strip, or directly to the wall. For accurate results, take all measurements using a metal tape measure.

ROLLER BLINDS

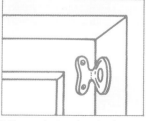

Roller blinds are as popular today as they were in Georgian and Victorian times. Their simple, unobtrusive lines are easily adaptable to both modern and traditional interiors, but they are particularly suitable for kitchens and bathrooms, where curtains are not always a practical solution.

The blind consists of flat, stiffened fabric secured to a wooden roller and hung from special brackets at each side of the window frame. A spring mechanism at one end of the roller allows the blind to be pulled up and down.

Although a roller blind works well on its own, it can look equally good with curtains, which need not function as such but merely consist of lengths of fabric caught back at the sides. Blinds are also good teamed with sheers for a more delicate effect. A shallow fabric pelmet can be fitted to hide a blind when it is not in use. For greater emphasis or to provide a border for a plain blind, accentuate the window frame with color or decorative stenciling.

Blind kits

Very easy to use, these come in two weights – standard, and heavy-duty for large windows. The basic kit consists of a wooden roller with a detachable cap and pin at one end, and a spring-winding mechanism at the other. The roller is available in various standard lengths, but can easily be sawn

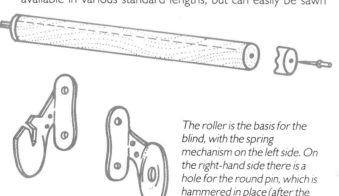

The roller is the basis for the blind, with the spring mechanism on the left side. On the right-hand side there is a hole for the round pin, which is hammered in place (after the roller has been cut to size) through a metal end cap.

Making a roller blind

1. Hammer the pin through hole in the cap. Do not rest the roller on the spring mechanism while hammering.

2. Screw the brackets in place at the window: the square-shaped bracket on the left and pin-hole bracket on the right.

Left: Simple roller blinds are often ideal for a room where the focus is elsewhere – dining for example. Their neutrality blends well with traditional or modern furniture.

down to give the precise length you need. Most rollers also have a guideline already marked along the length for attaching the fabric, but if not, then draw a line with a ruler before you begin to make the blind.

Also in the kit are brackets, which fit into a recessed window or at each side of a window, and a narrow wooden bar, which is slotted through the base of the blind to add weight and to help it hang well. The final component is a small pull cord attachment, which fits behind the lath.

Making a roller blind

Before taking any measurements, decide whether the blind is to hang inside or outside a recess and then establish the roller size. For a recessed window, measure the width of the recess exactly and deduct ⅝ inch at each side to allow for the roller fittings. For a window without a recess, where the blind is mounted on a window frame or wall, it is better to extend the measurements by about 1½ to 2 inches at the top and sides to prevent light showing around the edges. Trim roller to size, if needed, cover cut end with cap, and hammer pin in to secure it in position.

Before calculating the amount of fabric needed, the roller should be fixed in place. For fixing into a recess, screw the brackets 1¼ inches below the top of the recess, to allow for

the rolled-up blind (use anchors for fixing brackets to a wall), and slot in the correct size of roller.

For width of fabric needed, measure the length of the wooden roller (add ¾ inch for side hems for spray-stiffened fabric). For the length, measure from the top of the roller to the sill (or length needed) and add 12 inches to allow for the bottom hem casing and to make sure the roller is still covered when fully extended. Cut out making sure the edges are square and pattern repeats centred.

If using spray-stiffened fabric, turn a ⅜ inch hem down side edges. Zigzag stitch, centering stitching over raw edges.

For a plain bottom edge, make the casing for the wooden bar by folding over a 1½ to 2 inch double turning to the wrong side. Press and stitch across the casing. Press the fabric well and stiffen if needed. Slot the wooden bar through the casing and stitch to close. Screw down the cord pull to the center of the wooden bar, on the wrong side. With the fabric right side up, fold over and press a ¾ inch turning on the top edge. Place the roller on top with the spring mechanism to the left, and then tack the fabric edge to the guideline.

To make sure the winding mechanism is at the right tension, carefully roll up the blind by hand and insert it into the brackets. Pull the blind down as far as it will go. Check to see if it springs back to the top. If not, remove the blind and repeat.

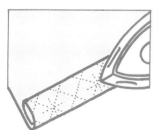 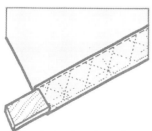 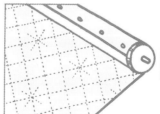 

3. Fold over double hem along the bottom edge of the blind to provide a casing in which to slot the wooden bar.

4. Slot the bar into the casing to stiffen the base of the blind. Slip-stitch each end of casing to hold bar.

5. Tack the top folded edge to the roller along marked line. Place the tacks at ¾ inch intervals with one at each end.

6. Thread cord through cord pull and screw to the center back of the wooden bar. Then thread through an "acorn".

Decorative edges

The hem or base of a roller blind need not be left plain. If the wooden bar is inserted slightly higher up the blind, the fabric below can be shaped into scallops, curves, zigzags or a crenellated edge where a decorative rod is slotted through loops in the bottom edge. You will need extra blind fabric for the facing. This should measure the width of the blind by about 5 inches wide.

For a shaped edge, you should use a stiffened fabric. First make the casing about 5 inches away from the bottom edge:

simply stitch a 1½ inch tuck in the fabric, press it flat towards the top and stitch along both edges. Apply the facing wrong sides together using fabric adhesive or double-sided iron-on interfacing. Then make a paper pattern as wide as the blind and 5 inches deep. Fold it concertina-wise into equal sections. Draw the required shape on the paper and cut out through all layers. Position pattern on the wrong side of blind and with a pencil lightly draw around. Carefully cut out. Stick trim over outer edge. Alternatively, you may prefer to close zigzag stitch around the edge before cutting out.

Scalloped edge

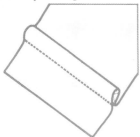

1. Stitch a 1½ inch tuck near to the base of the blind to form the casing for the wooden bar.

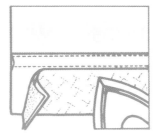

2. Fix facing in place to base of blind using double-sided iron-on bonding.

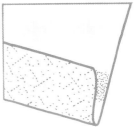

3. Fold up the paper concertina-wise and use a plate as a template.

4. Keeping the paper folded, carefully cut round the shaped edge, to form the pattern. Unfold paper pattern.

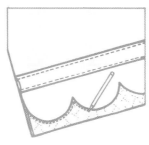

5. Place the paper to wrong side of blind below the wooden bar casing and mark round; cut out round the shaped edge.

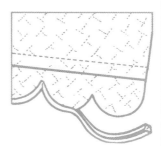

6. Fold trim evenly in half over the raw fabric edges and stick, or stitch in place, to neaten and finish the lower edge.

Crenellated edge

1. Fold back the facing to the wrong side of blind and stick, leaving a channel for the rod.

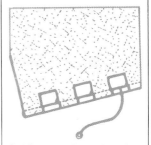

2. After completing the edge insert the rod and tie the cord and ring pull to the rod in the center of the blind.

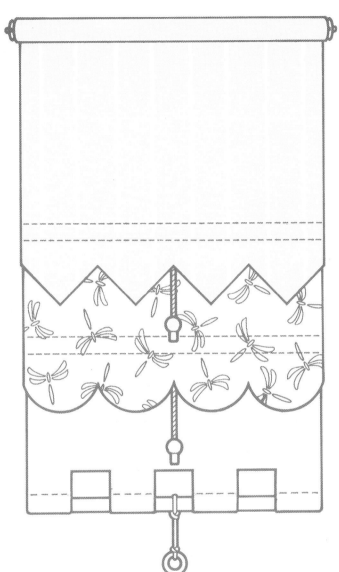

For a crenellated edge, a casing has to be made at the bottom for the rod. For the length of fabric needed, measure from the top of the roller to the sill and add 13 inches to include a 5 inch facing. Fold back the facing to the wrong side. Make and trace around the pattern and cut out, as before. Stick the facing to the back of the blind, leaving a 1½ to 2 inch casing for the rod. Slot the rod through the casing and knot the pull cord to the rod.

Twisted cord, braid or fringing can all be applied around the lower edge of the blind using clear fabric adhesive.

Above: Three popular roller blind finishes: zigzag, scallop and crenellated edge. Try to match the mood of the blind edge to the fabric. Divide up the edge so the shapes are evenly spaced across the blind.

Right: Blinds can be given a decorative edge to soften their somewhat utilitarian look. Here a shallow scalloped edging trimmed with white braid adds interest to a brightly colored, plain fabric roller blind.

ROMAN BLINDS

Roman blinds use less fabric than curtains and combine the softness of fabric with the neutral elegance of a flat surface. Small patterns, stripes or plains are best for their deep folds.

Roman blinds look newer and smarter than a roller blind. Requiring only a small amount of fabric, they pull up into softly folded pleats that look neat without being stark. Like roller blinds, they work well on their own or with draw curtains. These versatile blinds can be used in any room of the house, but choice of fabric is important. Many designs, particularly large round motifs, do not look good with the geometrical effect of the pleats. Both vertical and diagonal stripes, on the other hand, can look extremely smart – even quite dramatic, as can plain fabrics, or fabrics that have a definite texture.

Roman blinds are usually made from lined curtain fabric. This helps to keep out light and improves the shaping of the pleats. The blind is attached to a length of wooden battening, which is fixed into the recess of a window or above the window frame. Like roller blinds, Roman blinds are hung flat to the window with a wooden bar slotted through a casing in the lower hem, but pull up in the same way as festoon blinds. Cords are passed vertically through a series of rings attached to the back of the blind, and are knotted and held firmly on a cleat at the side of the window. Choose from either a narrow heading tape and slot through with split curtains rings, or use a special ringed tape which either combines tape and evenly spaced plastic rings or tape which contains cord rings, again spaced at regular intervals along the tape.

Making a Roman blind
Decide first whether your blind is to fit inside the window recess or outside the window frame; this will determine the length of the batten. If outside, the batten should be supported by brackets anchored into the wall.

To work out the width of fabric needed, measure the length of the batten and add 3½ inches for side turnings and seams. For the length, measure from the top of the batten to the sill and add 5 inches for hem casing and fixing to the batten. For the lining, measure as for the main fabric, less 3½ inches across the width.

You will also need a number of ringed tapes, depending on the width of the blind – tapes are spaced between 10 to 12 inches apart – each as long as the blind. For each tape, you

Making a Roman blind

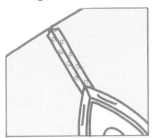

1. Join any fabric widths. Stitch fabric and lining together at side edges. Press seams.

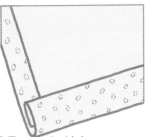

2. Turn up double hem at bottom edge and stitch across the blind twice to form a casing.

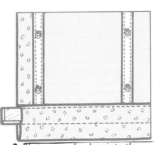

3. Slot a wooden bar into the casing and slip-stitch up both sides to hold firmly in place.

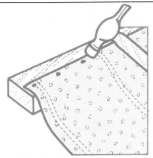

4. Fold both top edges of blind over the upper edge of the battening and fix in place.

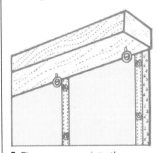

5. Fix a screw eye into the underside of the battening at the top of each row of tape.

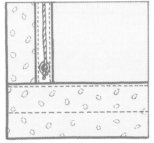

6. Tie cord to the bottom ring and thread up through all the rings above on each tape.

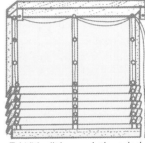

7. With all the cords threaded to one side, pull up together to raise or lower the blind.

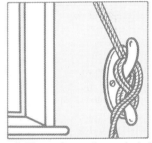

8. Tie cords together and wind them round the cleat in a figure-eight to hold the blind.

need a screw eye and cord. The amount of cord needed will be double the length of the finished blind plus the width measurement multiplied by the number of tapes used.

Trim or snip into the selvedges of the fabric and lining before cutting out the correct size and mark both centers at top and bottom with pins. With right sides facing, baste and machine-stitch ⅝ inch side seams. Press the seams open. Turn the blind to the right side. Match the center pins together at top and bottom of blind and press sides so seamlines will be 1¼ inches in from edges. On the bottom edge, with lining and fabric together, turn over ⅜ inch, then 4 inches to the wrong side, forming a casing, and pin.

Pin lengths of ringed or heading tape to the wrong side, beginning by covering the two seam lines and making sure the rings will align horizontally. Tuck the ends of the tape into the hem. Add more rows between, spacing them about 10 to 12 inches apart. Using a zipper foot, stitch the rows of tape down each side, through both layers of fabric. Stitch across the hem, catching in the ends of the tape, and stitch a second row about 1½ inches below, for the casing. Insert the lath to fit just inside the edges and slip-stitch both side edges to hold lath in position.

On the top edge, zigzag both fabrics together. Place ¾ inch over the top edge of the batten and tack or staple at 4 inch intervals. At the top of each tape, fix a screw eye into the underside of the batten.

THE CORDS Cut the cord into equal lengths and, beginning at the right-hand side, knot the cord to the first ring and thread up through the rings above. Continue to thread the cords through the screw eyes towards the left until all the cords are hanging together. Fix the blind to the window. Attach a cleat to the window frame about one-third up from the sill. Knot the cords together level with the sill, pull up the blind and wind the cords around the cleat to hold.

GATHERED BLINDS

Both festoon and Austrian blinds gather vertically into soft, luxurious folds and ruffles. These blinds could be lined and operate in a similar way to the Roman blind, with cords running through ringed or looped tapes stitched to the back. The Austrian blind is fuller than the festoon and constructed like a curtain with a heading tape and track. For either type of blind choose between narrow heading tape and split curtain rings or looped tape.

Festoon blinds

These are attached to the window in the same way as a Roman blind. For the length of fabric needed, measure from the batten to the sill and add one-third extra. For the width, measure the length of the batten plus 2½ inches for side turnings. Calculate the amount of tape, cord and screw eyes as for Roman blinds.

MAKING A FESTOON BLIND Make single 1¼ inches turnings on the side edges of the fabric, cover with tape and add more rows of tape in between, as for the Roman blind, making sure the rings or loops align horizontally. Stitch a double ¾ inch turning on the bottom of the blind, covering the tape ends. Fold over a ¾ inch turning on the top edge, and press. Loosen the cords just below the turning and pull up each tape until the blind fits the window. Even the gathers. Wind the excess cords into small bows and knot securely. Fix to the batten and finish as for Roman blind.

Austrian blinds

Flounced and frilly, Austrian blinds pull up into softly gathered swags, and usually hang fairly low in the window from a gathered heading.

The blind is either gathered onto a pole or fixed to the window on a batten, with a standard curtain track and runners fitted to the front edge. Calculate the amount of fabric needed in the same way as you would for a festoon blind but allow twice the width. If using a frill allow twice the fabric width by 5½ inches deep. Calculate the amount of narrow heading, or looped tape, cord and screw eyes as for the Roman blind.

Austrian and festoon blinds work well in a wide range of fabrics and prints. Here, a plain creamy-white Austrian blind has been chosen as a discreet but stylish window treatment.

Making an Austrian blind

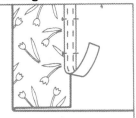

1. Turn in 1 ¼ inches down each side. Stitch heading tape over raw edges. Stitch extra tapes across the blind.

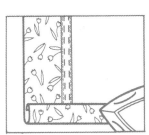

2. Turn over a 1 ¼ inch hem at the base of the blind and tuck under ⅜ inch. Stitch, catching down tape.

3. At the top, turn over 5 inches, tuck under ⅜ inch. Stitch along fold and again 3 inches above for casing.

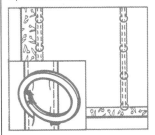

4. Slip split rings through tape pockets, with first row ¾ inch from hem edge. Pull up each tape, if desired.

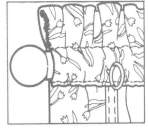

5. Thread pole through top casing, adding end finials. Fix screw eyes into base of pole at the top of each tape row.

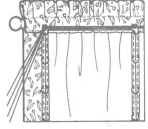

6. Knot first length of cord to first ring then up through all the rings above and screw eyes to one side. Repeat.

MAKING AN AUSTRIAN BLIND Make a single 1 ¼ inch turning on the side edges of the blind fabric and around the frill, leaving the top edge free. Pin the tape over the raw edges and then pin the remaining tapes at equal intervals across the blind, as for the Roman blind. If using a frill, run gathering threads through top of frill, match to bottom edge of blind and stitch right sides together. Turn over raw edge to neaten. Alternatively, turn up ⅝ inch then 1 inch to make a hem. If using a pole, follow instructions above. Or apply heading tape and thread on hooks, as for unlined curtain. Complete by slotting the hooks into the runners.

LOUVERS AND PLEATED BLINDS

Above: Vertical louver blinds are usually associated with office spaces, but they can look stylish in a home. As the louvers can be angled, they suit a sunny room with a good view where privacy is also needed.

Right: Louvered shutters have a slightly colonial feeling, and make attractive additions to rooms furnished with natural materials where a patterned fabric window covering would look out of place.

Vertical louver blinds are usually associated with offices but they can often be very effective in other locations. They consist of thin strips of fabric, usually acrylic or polyester, but sometimes rough silk, or even a stiffened sheer, attached to tracks at the top and bottom of the window. They pivot open and shut and can be drawn to one side. They are also good room dividers, especially in floor-to-ceiling lengths. They can also come fitted inside double glazing and mechanically operated from inside the room but only in specially made windows. They are often used where curtains would not be appropriate, such as a conservatory, office-type room or study. However, they should not be totally dismissed for use in living rooms, bedrooms and bathrooms, since they can look very effective when used in the right location.

Louvered shutters can be bought in plain wood from a range of standard widths and lengths, and are fitted by means of hinged brackets. They work very well on many types of window, and can be attractive features on tall windows, either in plain or stained wood, or painted to coordinate with the rest of the room. Used on French windows or as room dividers they retain a feeling of spaciousness while providing a certain amount of privacy.

Pleated blinds are usually made from tough, super-smoothed paper or fiber, in permanent narrow pleats. They are inexpensive and come in a good but limited choice of colors and patterns. They exclude light well, provide some insulation, are very easy to install and pull up to fit neatly into the window reveal allowing a curtain track to be fixed above. Used without curtains, they are perfect for awkward roof windows or conservatories. An occasional dusting will keep them looking good for a long time.

Perforated blinds These crisply pleated blinds are made from tough, specially treated paper, punched with holes to allow light to filter through. They are cheap and traditional in appearance and are becoming increasingly popular for window coverings in workrooms and conservatories.

SLATTED BLINDS

Slatted blinds come in several sizes and a few colors, but mostly in natural wood shades, which give a soft, mellow warmth to a room. Because they are relatively cheap to buy and easy to put up, they are a popular answer to furnishing temporary accommodation. They not only look good as window coverings or room dividers but they also keep out a fair degree of light and can easily be taken down when the time comes to move on.

Cane blinds are cheap and made from natural-colored split bamboo, whole bamboo or rattan or plain wood painted to look like bamboo. The blinds are usually rolled up by means of cords, but there is also a variety that pulls up in loose pleats. Cane blinds look good inside a window with a deep reveal, and are especially practical in kitchens and bathrooms if there is no problem of being in direct view. They also make excellent room dividers and can be used as screens for storage areas.

Wooden blinds consist of thin strips of wood closely woven together, made up and operated in the same way as cane blinds. They usually come in natural wood colors, or a fine

Slatted blinds always evoke the pleasures of open-air living in hot climates.

Far left: A covered terrace may not be entirely practical, but the idea can be easily adapted for a pretty, temporary summer patio cover.

Left: That oriental atmosphere has been successfully imported for a beautiful interior that combines Eastern and antique elements beautifully. Raw silk curtains over the slatted blinds are an ideal combination.

dark green traditionally used in conservatories, but there is no reason why they should not be sprayed any color.

Wooden blinds do not exclude daylight totally, but when they are pulled down, the diffused light that filters through is very pleasing. They are usually quite cheap, and come in specific sizes, although there are some firms who will make them up to suit the customers' own requirements.

Matchstick blinds are made from very thin strips of pale split cane, woven together with cotton and taped at the edges. They can be bought in fairly wide widths and are especially useful for windows in sloping ceilings and other inaccessible places. They either roll up like cane blinds or pull up like Roman blinds.

Plastic strips A modern version of the old wooden bars, these blinds, made from narrow strips of plastic, have a fresh, light appearance and work well in rooms that have a predominance of colored rather than wooden surfaces, such as kitchens, bathrooms and lavatories. They are also easy to keep clean – just an occasional wipe with a damp cloth is all they require.

VENETIAN BLINDS

Venetian blinds (originally office fittings) have found a place in many contemporary interiors. The slats can be made of aluminum, wood or plastic. The aluminum slats are available in every color imaginable, including black, white, gold and silver. They can be made to order to fit any window from the smallest pane to floor-to-ceiling sheets of glass, and come in various widths, the smartest and least obtrusive being the very narrow slats, which are almost impossible to discern when the blind is opened.

The Venetian blind is a versatile window covering: it can be fully raised, lowered with the slats open to provide light but almost total privacy or lowered with the slats closed to give complete privacy, total light exclusion, and a fair degree of insulation. They are, however, fairly difficult to clean – a boisterous brushing can turn half of the slats upside down, while too soft a wipe will leave most of the dust behind. A regular feather-dusting is probably the best answer, or try a sponge dipped in soapy water for very dirty blinds. Some companies will dismantle and remove your blinds for professional cleaning.

Both metal and plastic Venetian blinds can be made to order in a wide selection of colors, with matching cords, head and bottom rails. You can also have blinds made up in more than one color. Some are fitted with Plexiglas rods instead of cords, which makes the overall effect more transparent when the blinds are open.

Although Venetian blinds were originally designed to fit very wide windows and primarily those in modern interiors, they work equally well in more classically decorated rooms. The color range is extremely wide and ranges from pastels and primaries through to darker colors such as deep red, fir green and chocolate brown.

Wooden Venetian blinds are usually made from pine or Western red cedar for strength and lightness, and are generally operated by a single cord, rod and handle. Some types are also available that are powered by an electric motor. Although they cost more than their metal or plastic counterparts, the expense is more than justified since they should last a lifetime.

Two interiors convey the vast range of effects you can find in Venetian blinds.
Far left: Shiny blue plastic blinds make a bold statement against a sloping window.

Below: Wooden Venetian blinds cost more than plastic, but have the warmth and simplicity that make them ideal for a modern setting where natural materials dominate.

INDEX

Acknowledgments

The publishers would like to thank: The John Lewis Partnership; Alexander Furnishings

Illustrators: Terry Evans; Coral Mula; Elsa Wilson

Picture credits:
Abbreviations: CO – Conran Octopus Ltd; EWA – Elizabeth Whiting & Associates; *MMC – La Maison de Marie Claire; WOI – The World of Interiors*

Michael Boys 25; Camera Press 6-7, 12-13, 13, 14 left, 15 right, 29, 31, 33 left, 34, 55, 68, 72-3, 76; *Cent Idées*/Alex MacLean 58-9; Collier Campbell 18; CO/John Heseltine 38-9; EWA/David Cripps 57; EWA/Michael Dunne 15 left, 20; EWA/Clive Helm 30; EWA/Spike Powell 14 right; EWA/Tim Street-Porter 77; EWA/Jerry Tubby 19; *Good Housekeeping*/ Jan Baldwin 47; Susan Griggs Agency/Michael Boys 9, 16, 32, 35; Habitat 11, 22-3, 27, 33 right, 58, 59, 60-1, 61, 72; *MMC*/Claude Pataut 26; *MMC*/Jean-Luc Eriaud 74; Bill McLaughlin 70-1; Merloni Casa 8; Sunway Blinds 67; *WOI*/ Richard Bryant 24; *WOI*/Clive Frost 49, 62-3; *WOI*/Tom Leighton 75; *WOI*/James Mortimer 17, 21, 28-9, 37; *WOI*/ Karen Radkai 48; *WOI*/James Wedge 60